THE
ENERGY BUS

FIELD GUIDE

JON GORDON
WITH AMY P. KELLY

WILEY

Library of Congress Cataloging-in-Publication Data:

Names: Gordon, Jon, 1971- author. | Kelly, Amy, author.
Title: The energy bus field guide / Jon Gordon, with Amy Kelly.
Description: Hoboken, New Jersey : John Wiley & Sons, Inc., [2018] |
    Identifiers: LCCN 2017044988 (print) | LCCN 2017049994 (ebook) | ISBN 9781119412465 (pdf) |
    ISBN 9781119412489 (epub) | ISBN 9781119412458 (pbk.)
Subjects: LCSH: Teams in the workplace–Management. | Employee motivation. |
    Motivation (Psychology) | Positive psychology. | Success.
Classification: LCC HD66 (ebook) | LCC HD66 .G67155 2018 (print) | DDC 658.4/022–dc23
LC record available at https://lccn.loc.gov/2017044988

Printed in the United States of America

SKY10041873_012623

Table of Contents

Introduction

Why a Field Guide?

I know from personal experience that taking a ride on the Energy Bus can change the entire course of your life, and on some level, you already believe that too. You made a decision to experience the benefits of positive energy in your life through the rules in the Energy Bus book, and this field guide will help build upon that experience.

I wrote *The Energy Bus* to help you take action toward more positive outcomes for your life, work, and team. This field guide complements the book by providing additional resource materials, specific practical guidance, and workbook-style content that further enables you to implement the 10 rules in *The Energy Bus* in your life, team, and organization.

From the moment *The Energy Bus* was published, readers have been clamoring for more information on how to implement the ideas outlined in the book. I have been writing newsletters, speaking all over the world, creating training materials, and answering personal emails in a continuous effort to provide support to individuals, teams, and organizations working with the book and seeing remarkable, positive results. When asking one of the leaders that implemented the program so successfully at her organization about the process for her success, she said, "Based on my experience in learning and development, I knew reading the book alone wouldn't cut it. We had to live it somehow to get it to work." This comment started my thinking about other ways to help the individuals that wanted to make the rules in the book come alive in their personal life and work.

As supplemental materials for the book continued to grow exponentially and become more diverse, I realized it would be helpful to pull them all together into one comprehensive tool. I wanted to create a one-stop shop for you to begin your own Energy Bus journey.

Who Should Read This Field Guide?

This field guide is designed to help anyone interested in turning the 10 rules in *The Energy Bus* into reality in their day-to-day life. It is for anyone who wants to live and work with more vision, optimism, passion, and purpose. It is for executives, managers, coaches, teachers, parents, volunteers, community leaders, church leaders, healthcare professionals, trainers, facilitators, team builders, and students.

If you want to flourish personally and to help others around you do the same, this field guide will help you maximize every part of the journey through vivid individual and group activities that link back to one of the 10 rules in the book. I call them the "Ten Rules for the Ride of Your Life."

How to Use This Book

Like *The Energy Bus*, this field guide follows a simple, powerful approach as well. It is a practical guide to support you in implementing the principles in the book. Each chapter presents information to help make the rules come alive in a logical order that mirrors the book. I designed this field guide to help you do three things:

1. Implement the Energy Bus principles in your own life.
2. Utilize these principles with your team.
3. Share ideas, case studies, and best practices to help you create an Energy Bus initiative in your organization.

This field guide is my gift to you. It is a summary of everything I have seen and learned thus far about how to successfully implement the Energy Bus in your life, your team, and your organization. There is not one specific way to do this. The exciting thing about *The Energy Bus* is how people have used so many creative approaches to make positive changes—and knowing there are more to come.

As you work through this process, feel free to implement your own creative ideas. You may want to use this field guide for just your own life. Or you may decide to invite your team on the bus. Or, like many others, you may decide to create an Energy Bus program in your organization. I've worked to pull together materials that can help you build the road map for whatever journey you want to take and, as the driver, you decide what kind of ride it's going to be.

I look forward to hearing about your story and the things you do to implement *The Energy Bus*. If you decide to share it with your team and organization, I would love to hear from you. You can email me at info@JonGordon.com. Who knows, your story may be in the next addition of the field guide. As you embark on this journey, please know I am sending positive energy your way.

The Case for Positive Energy

Positive Energy is an undeniably powerful asset as well as a vital personal and organizational resource. It has fueled many successful people and organizations, and those who see positive energy in action recognize it and usually want to be a part of it.

I have witnessed it personally through my work with *The Energy Bus*, and I am certain you have experienced it too. Let's face it: You need energy to accomplish any activity. Teams and organizations need energy to accomplish their goals. And most people agree that where there is positive energy, productivity is higher, teamwork is improved, and joy fills the process.

If you have ever been around someone who is negative, you know it. You know, the guy that complains and never has anything good to say about anyone, or that individual with the huge scowl on her face who rolls her eyes at anyone's ideas. You don't want to be around those people. You want to be around positive energy and generally recoil from the negative. And guess what? You are not alone. Positive energy is a commodity in high demand, and this field guide is a road map on how to create it in abundance to fuel personal, team, and organizational success.

More and more research shows that you either draw positive or negative energy from the people you interact with daily, and that energy can either fuel success or contribute to personal or organizational decline. Most people do not want to be negative, and many proven health and organizational benefits emerge when individuals focus on positive energy. Some of the health benefits linked to positive energy include: a longer life span, lower stress, lower rates of depression, increased resistance to the common cold, better stress management and coping skills, lower risk of cardiovascular disease-related death, increased physical well-being, and better psychological health. All these things are beneficial to you, your family, and your teams. In addition, organizations and teams with positive energy have been linked to increased engagement, morale, productivity, and, ultimately, increased revenue and profitability. Positivity is also present in organizations with lower attrition and absenteeism. These organizations are also known to have more *fun*. I've seen it all over the world. People want more positive energy and the proven benefits that come with it.

Productivity has been shown to skyrocket in an atmosphere of positivity. This is true for individuals and groups. Remember that wherever you go, there you are. You have to be around yourself all the time, and people that complain or focus on the negative are generally people that say they are depressed or unhappy. If there is positive energy at home or at work, chances are you feel more engagement, more joy, and more overall well-being. Higher engagement and well-being generally translates into higher performance, and that is what you want personally and professionally. For all these reasons and many more, I created this field guide to help you bring positive energy into your personal life and organization through the rules in *The Energy Bus*.

Positive energy is the best preparation for any skepticism, and skepticism can actually lead to the perfect environment for making a difference. Even though we know positive energy makes a difference, some individuals, CEOs, and coaches I have spoken with say their first introduction to a "book about a bus" was not embraced immediately. Even with all the research and many practical examples in most people's lives, you can still encounter skepticism about positive energy. Some people are unsure about *The Energy Bus* being a credible answer to improving their team or organization.

However, the positive results speak for themselves. Many of the individuals who tell me these exciting turnaround stories are featured in this field guide or in my talks related to the amazing changes and results in their lives, teams, and companies. It is hard to argue with the research that supports positivity, and most importantly, the many success stories people have shared with me. The mounting examples of changed lives and the overwhelming positive momentum for the book speak for themselves.

Bringing more positive energy into the world is my personal mission, and this field guide is a reference tool to take the proven benefits of positive energy to others. Rule #3 in *The Energy Bus* is to "Fuel Your Ride with Positive Energy," and this field guide helps you take the proven power of positive energy directly into your personal life, team, and organization to get the same results.

A Quick Overview of the "Ten Rules for the Ride of Your Life"

Before you get started, please review the rules below. These are the rules from the book that the main character, George, learns from Joy the bus driver and other characters on her Energy Bus. These are the rules that forever change George's life and the lives of his team members.

This field guide will help you bring the rules to life in your Energy Bus program. The reflection questions, team-building activities, and organizational program ideas in the guide are designed to support each rule, and you can make the decisions on how to combine them in the best way to achieve your vision for the road ahead. You are the driver of your bus, and I am excited to support you in having the ride of your life.

1. You're the driver of your bus.

2. Desire, vision, and focus move your bus in the right direction.

3. Fuel your ride with positive energy.

4. Invite people on your bus and share your vision for the road ahead.

5. Don't waste your energy on those who don't get on your bus.

6. Post a sign that says "No Energy Vampires Allowed."

7. Enthusiasm attracts more passengers and energizes them during the ride.

8. Love your passengers.

9. Drive with purpose.

10. Have fun and enjoy the ride.

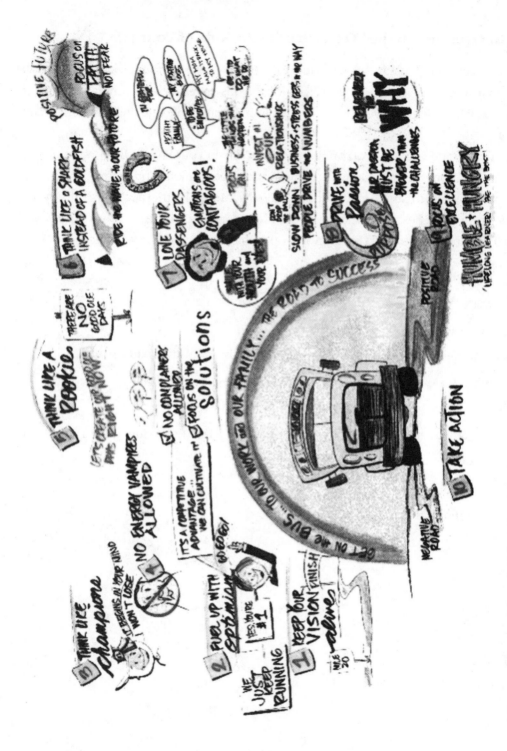

One reader's artwork of all the Energy Bus Rules for The Ride of Your Life

The Case for Positive Energy

Rule 1

You're the Driver of Your Bus

In a time and world where we deal with so many negative things and people,
The Energy Bus *beautifully articulates the power of positive energy and attitude.*
The book will change your life and teach you how to be the driver of your bus.
Buckle up and ENJOY the ride!

—Dabo Swinney, Head Coach, Clemson University Football Team

Becoming the driver of your bus is the first rule for the ride of your life, and it is where you need to start. You have to take responsibility for your life to drive in the right direction toward your goals and dreams. When you take control of your bus, you gain the ability to take it where you want to go. The problem today is that people often feel like they have no say in where their bus is going or how it is going to get there. The first step in the Energy Bus process is to become the driver of your own bus, because, without this step, you won't be the one driving and charting the course for success. Becoming a driver is your choice. It is a decision that you make, and it is one of promise and purpose. The decision to become a driver is what sets you on the road to your personal goals. It is one that I have taken and it is one that I've seen many others take as a start to an incredible new future.

This rule is the first step because, without a driver, you cannot go anywhere at all—and when you choose to be the driver, all things are possible. This decision is empowering, and it is an immediate catalyst to create positive energy. As a driver, you take the wheel, set the course for the road ahead, and begin an amazing journey.

? Who Is the Driver of Your Bus?

Complete the questions below.

1. What does being the driver of your bus mean to you?

_____

_____

_____

2. What qualities do you think make a good driver?

_____

_____

_____

3. Can you recall a time when you weren't a driver and blamed others for the circumstances of your life? How did it feel?

_____

_____

_____

4. True or false? I can take responsibility for my life and have the power to create the life that I want.

_____

_____

_____

5. How will making the decision to be a driver impact you, the people around you, and your work?

_____

_____

_____

6. What are some actions you can take to demonstrate the role of driver?

_____

_____

_____

A Team of Drivers

To create a successful life, you must realize that you are the driver of your bus, and to create a successful team you must have a fleet of drivers. It's important to have each person on the bus and also to be driving the bus forward. This goes for work teams as well as family teams. We have heard from many families that have become drivers together, and the results have been exciting and transformative. If you want to bring

The Energy Bus to your family or team, you must help them understand that they play an essential role. Their attitude and actions are crucial to success. They need to become a team of drivers.

To start developing a team of drivers, I recommend sharing *The Energy Bus* with your team and giving them the opportunity to familiarize themselves with the 10 rules. You can get a book for each team member or get a few books to share. A few members of the team can read them, sign their names inside when they finish, and then pass the books on to the next group of team members. Once everyone has read it, then you can do a few team-building exercises to bring Rule #1 to life.

You're the Driver: Team-Building Activities

Drivers Wanted Advertisement

If you had to create a "drivers wanted" ad for your team, what would it say? Design the ad on a poster board and share it with your team. Explain the choices you made. This can be an excellent individual or team activity. Get a group together and hand out small or large poster board. The team can work together as a whole or work in small table groups. Ask them to make "drivers wanted" ads that contain the characteristics drivers need. The individuals or groups can share their work and discuss what matters most to the team.

Driver Interview

Ask your team to find a partner. This activity asks the participants to interview one another for a bus driver position. What questions would you ask? What qualities and competencies would be important? What type of driver would you look for to motivate you and bring the right kind of energy and culture to your team? Is a driver a leader? Why and how? At the end of the interview activity, the different pairs report out to the group on the questions they asked, the qualities they were looking for, and why those characteristics would be important for team and organization success. The facilitator makes a master list of qualities and questions. Then the facilitator asks the group "should anything else be added to our list?"

Some companies and teams have used this activity to evaluate the questions team members come up with and consider how these questions may be important in the hiring profile of new teammates or new members of the organization. The resulting list is a great resource to evaluate the type of culture needed for team success and to further refine the hiring profile for talent scouts for the team.

Bus Driver Scavenger Hunt

Give each person on your team one or two bus driver cards containing the Energy Bus rules. Bus driver cards can be index cards that say "Bus Driver Scavenger Hunt" on one side, and have one of the 10 rules of the Energy Bus on the other side. Each person also gets a bus driver roster. This is a piece of paper with two columns. One column has the 10 rules from *The Energy Bus*, and the other column is blank. To complete the scavenger hunt, each person must complete the blank column, using the process that follows.

Tell everyone in the room to get up and move among the different people in the group, asking each other what rule they have on their bus driver card and what it means to them. As the attendees do this, have them complete a full bus driver roster. As people talk to others in the room, they write each person's name next to the rule he or she has on their bus driver card. The participants also learn about what each rule means to the person carrying it. The bus driver roster must have a person's name next to each rule to win the scavenger hunt. The first person to get all 10 rules on their roster wins the Bus Driver Scavenger Hunt. After the activity is complete, ask the team what they noticed during the scavenger hunt. What stuck out to them about what their team members said about the rules? What new insights did they have personally that related to the 10 rules? Does the team feel like they have a better understanding and knowledge of the 10 rules? Are they ready to become drivers?

Or you can do this one:

Rule Presentation

Break up the team into pairs and assign each pair one or two of the rules, depending on the size of your team, and have the pair present the rule to the rest of the team. You could make a song, commercial, poem, rap, short speech, or other creative piece to share the rule. This activity gives your team the opportunity to start getting used to driving. They are starting to set the tone for how the rules in the book can be applied to team success.

An Organization Filled with Drivers

As I mentioned in the beginning of this guide, one of my goals with this field guide is to share best practices of how people and organizations have utilized *The Energy Bus*. Regarding Rule #1, You're the Driver of Your Bus, having an organization of people who understand their roles in creating a positive organization and are willing to act as a foundational component to organizational success is essential to a culture filled with drivers of positive energy and positive outcomes. The more your teams embrace the idea of becoming positive drivers, the stronger your odds of accomplishing your goals.

The case study, "United Parcel Service of America," includes a few ideas of how entire organizations have created drivers. I've also included various best practices of various organizations as well.

 Case Study: United Parcel Service of America

The Energy Bus was implemented at UPS. To get started, the book was given to 1,000 leaders. Nancy Koeper, President of the UPS Northwest District, said, "I was looking for something to unify and connect the workforce. A colleague suggested *The Energy Bus*. After reading it and feeling energized, I couldn't help but feel this would help me accomplish what I needed to. I personally distributed a copy to each person on my team and wrote a note in each book. I asked them to read it within the month and send me a note to share their thoughts on how they were going to begin incorporating the book's concepts into their lives and [those of] the people they lead. We have seen improved morale, performance, ownership of results, increased discretionary effort, and more inspired leadership."

To further evaluate results, at the start of the program, engagement, absenteeism, and morale were measured to establish the baseline. Once the program was launched, the concepts in the book were reinforced through a consistent communication plan via email, video, and job aids.

After the program and concepts of positivity in the book were implemented, absenteeism went down, engagement went up, and morale improved significantly. This all started with asking everyone to begin with Rule #1.

 **Best Practices**

Launch Events

I have learned that companies have had a lot of success by introducing *The Energy Bus* with a launch event. For example, some organizations have called the launch event "Positive Drivers Wanted." Some organizations give out the book at the launch event, and some provide the books in advance. Some companies buy a few books and create a shared library for everyone to check out the book and return it for others to use. Another reference for your launch event could be the free resource poster with the 10 rules on it, found in the Driver's Kit that is available at www.theenergybus.com/kit.html. The critical step in launching an Energy Bus program and gaining alignment is to expose the team to the content and the rules and have them make the decision to become a driver.

On the one hand, I've worked with companies that said, "Just read the book" to their teams, and did nothing to reinforce the concepts. On the other hand, some organizations really embraced the book, reinforced the principles, and engaged in the types of activities I've included in this field guide. The organizations that took the time to communicate consistently, create alignment, and reinforce through activities and messaging are the organizations where I have observed the most impactful success. Those teams and organizations are the ones that became filled with positive drivers that moved the program forward. Those groups made the rules come alive through their events, messaging, and activities. Again, their results are why this field guide exists.

 Case Study: Energy Rally

One organization held an Energy Rally to launch their program. People came to a vibrant meeting in the company's event center and got an overview of the 10 rules from the book. Then they were asked to break into small groups and talk about the value of positivity in their workplace and share real-life examples of ways they could bring more positive energy to their own teams. This was a simple approach, and it worked very well.

Drivers of Weekly or Monthly Meetings

You might consider launching an Energy Bus program in your company by having one member of the team share and facilitate a discussion around of one the rules each week or month. For the first meeting, share an overview of the Energy Bus, and then you can begin with Rule #1. This practice can also be reinforced on a broader scale with monthly emails to the entire organization, highlighting a rule and the leader's thoughts about how the rule is valuable and impacting the team in a positive way. Store these weekly/monthly messages in a shared location for the team's ongoing use.

Drivers as Future Leaders

Some companies created teams with each team having a driver over certain portions of the road map for success. These drivers became leaders in the talent succession pipeline and grew and developed significantly through the process.

You may want to consider assigning a team of people to each rule in the book to make sure the energy and focus stay alive for each rule as the program moves forward. There could be a driver for each of these Energy Committees, and this position could end up being a leadership opportunity as well. The drivers of the Energy Committees work together through collaboration and communication to help integrate the rules for maximum overall program success. If you decide to take this approach with your program, you can ask people to volunteer for the Energy Committee driver roles, or you could assign this opportunity to up-and-coming mid-level leaders.

Case Study: The Planes Companies

John Sabatalo, President at The Planes Companies, decided to launch an Energy Bus program at the same time the leadership team had been working on an initiative to redefine the company's vision and core principles. The team had been meeting weekly for close to three months, and after much deliberation, established a new set of core principles centered on the acronym of TEAM: trust, empowerment, accountability, mesh. With the core principles decided, the conversation turned to the question: What would be the most effective way to launch the new core principles to the organization? After a series of discussions, they decided to launch a monthly leadership series for department leaders and above. The leadership series would focus on the new core principles of TEAM and use *The Energy Bus* as a type of curriculum tool to bring a much higher level of energy, purpose, and vision to the organization. John made it clear that he wanted to see employees embrace the principles, particularly the concept that they were drivers and had to make that decision for the program to be a success.

The complete case study of the Planes Company is included in the Additional Case Studies section of this Field Guide.

Chief Energy Officer (CEO)

While launching the program and recruiting drivers, another important step many teams and companies have shared is to make sure that the top leader of the team or organization believes in the program and will stand behind it in words and actions. Positive leadership at the top is a critical component to success.

Chief Energy Officer, Ken Fisher, CEO of Fisher Investments, said, "The concept of the chief energy officer teaches us that attitude alignment isn't just linear but a non-linear leap that makes the ultimate difference between abundance or lack of happiness, success, performance, motivation, ability to be team oriented, and our reality of achieving our personal goals in all parts of our lives."

The president, coach, principal, CEO, parent, or whoever is the head of the organization is a very special kind of driver. This person is usually designated as the CEO (chief energy officer) and is responsible for helping to reinforce the rules in the book by embodying them through their own leadership behavior. You do not have to make the company president or head of the team the chief energy officer, but I do recommend reading the sample job description and considering how the leader of the organization or team will consistently communicate the vision, reinforce the rules, and fuel the team with positive energy. There is a sample chief energy officer job description to use in your program planning included in the resource section of this field guide.

Rule 2

Desire, Vision, and Focus Move Your Bus in the Right Direction

If you can see it, you can create it. If you have a vision, then you also have the power to make it happen.

"Where am I going?" It seems like a simple question, but if you do not have a clear answer, there is no way to be a driver that is headed in the right direction. Every driver needs a vision, the outcome you are driving toward. There is power in a vision to create your future. A clear, positive vision will help you move the bus in the right direction and give power to your purpose and focus to your mission.

In Rule #1, you decided to become the driver of your bus, and that step is empowering. Your thoughts and vision are the steering wheel that will guide your bus where you want it to go. Now you need to take the next step toward that destination. Getting there will take proper, positive steering that is directed by desire, vision, and focus. Here is why each of these three elements is important:

1. **Desire:** Your desire represents how earnest you are about achieving your vision. Desire helps you determine just how badly you want it and it makes you hungry to see your own success.

2. **Vision:** Vision is looking ahead to the future and breathing actual life into it. Vision takes your one-dimensional desire and turns it into a three-dimensional, fully animated motion picture of your goal. Vision gives you the ability to see yourself having already reached your goal and empowers the intention of taking it from a dream into reality.

3. **Focus:** Focus is setting your aim, and then directing your attention and actions purposefully on the goals you defined. Focus is where you block out the distractions and make a commitment to the future achievement of the vision. When you are focused, you look ahead at the goal through your bus's windshield. You are not concerned with the rearview mirror. You set your sights on the road ahead and drive.

Every journey starts with a desire to go somewhere. Desire, vision, and focus are the elements that guide you on a successful journey. Without these three elements, your bus will not end up at your desired destination. So, grab the wheel, put those elements into practice, and move your bus exactly where you want it to go.

? Consider Your Desire, Vision, and Focus

Complete the questions below.

1. What is your vision for your life?

_____

_____

_____

2. What is your vision for your work, job, and career?

_____

_____

_____

3. What action steps do you need to take to realize your visions?

_____

_____

_____

4. How committed are you to the vision you have for the future? What are you willing to do to get there? How deep is your desire?

_____

_____

_____

5. Desire, vision, or focus: Which is your strongest point?

_____

_____

_____

6. Desire, vision, or focus: Which is your biggest opportunity to improve?

_____

_____

_____

7. What steps will you take to improve?

_____

_____

_____

8. What specific steps will you take to stay focused on your goals?

_____

_____

_____

9. How can you document and display your vision for the future in your day-to-day life, so that you can keep your desire fueled and your focus sharp?

_____

_____

_____

A Team Vision

If you have a vision, you also have the power to make it happen. You have probably heard the statement, "If you can dream it, you can achieve it." While this is true, the additional elements required for the attainment of your vision, or dream, are the desire and focus necessary to keep you on course.

This works in your life and with your team as well. When it comes to teams, clarity of the destination is even more important. When communicating with a group, the specificity of the vision has to reach beyond your own understanding and encompass where the group wants to go. The vision needs to be clear, so you can share the destination and move in the same direction together. You must have a defined team vision to accomplish team goals.

One way to create a group vision is on your own, but most teams get members of their group together to discuss what they need to do and chart a course using team input. Bringing the team together to create the vision is a best practice that I support. It is a proven approach to drive maximum clarity, alignment, and collaboration. If you get the team involved in creating the vision, research says they will buy in more and be more motivated to contribute in order to achieve it.

When John Sabatalo, CEO of The Planes Companies, was thinking about what to do for his team during the annual planning process, he asked his wife whether she thought he should give the people on his company's leadership team *The Energy Bus* book. She said, "If you want your team to play in the Super Bowl, then have them read it. If you don't want them to even make the playoffs, then don't have them read it." I share this with you, because reading the book prior to finalizing the vision with the team can provide a big advantage.

 ## Creating the Vision: Team-Building Activities

Create the Vision

Bring your team together, and ask the question "Do we have a clear vision for where we are going?" Facilitate the discussion, and ask each member of the team to share their personal vision for the future and/or their perspective on where the team is going. Ask the group "What are we doing today that pushes us toward our vision and goals, and what may we need to stop doing?" This activity is a great way to gain clarity around the organization or team vision and promote positive communication in the group. You can uncover significant opportunities and also identify things that the group believes are not contributing to success. It is a best practice to keep detailed notes during these team sessions or to ask the team if you can record the sessions and then get the discussion transcribed for a group reference.

Make a Mural to Show Desire, Vision, and Focus

Find a wall in your organization's team space that is prominently visible. Have the team create a vision mural. This can be a place to put the organization's overall vision in the center of the mural and support that vision with artwork and/or inspirational quotes from the team around the vision, or it can be a place to have the overall vision surrounded by team members' personal goals and commitments for the success of the program. No matter how you choose to execute this activity, it is designed to provide a visual representation of the defined vision and reinforce the focus on the vision on a consistent basis. By having the team work together to complete the mural, you will know that they are all connected to the vision in a tangible way.

Desire and Focus

Once you have a clear vision, many times it can be valuable to have the team complete an activity answering the questions: How can we keep the desire and focus high as we drive toward our vision? What are some ways we can motivate the team and support them to stay on track for success? These questions can be answered individually and then shared with the group. Finally, the group can pick the top one to three ideas and implement practices or programs for the road ahead.

An Organizational Vision

If you are someone who wants to share the power of a vision with your entire organization, there are a number of visions you can have. One company had a goal of $1 billion in sales. That was where they were driving, and that vision provided the team with the ability to choose actions that aligned their focus with that vision. Another organization had a vision to create a more positive culture and a more positive team environment, which takes a lot of drivers all heading in the same direction.

Case Study: Sharing the Vision and Developing Leaders
Liz Hall, Training and Development Executive, C & A Industries

One company's vision was to create the next group of company leaders. The head of the learning and development organization said:

I had so many demands for team leader training. This is the first-layer leadership position in our company, and the executive team had a vision to train 70 people in one year. I did not have the resources to train all the individuals that needed to be trained. I had to come up with a way to bring this book and its message into the workplace and find a way to offer leadership training to a group of about 70 people. The idea to merge them together came to me, seriously, at 3 a.m. one morning. I had just re-read the book and loved the concept of a CEO (chief energy officer), but I decided to give it a different twist.

I thought with a group this size I could form teams (buses), and each team could have a CEO (bus driver, team leader, or team leader-to-be). We could work through the book and impact the entire company's goals, and provide leadership opportunities at the same time. We formed 11 teams of 8 to 10 people. I gave the criteria for what we were looking for in drivers (e.g., wanted to advance in the company, lead a group, etc.), and I selected 11 drivers. These drivers helped carry the vision of the program to their teams and others in the organization. People knew that we wanted proactive people that were willing to take on assignments to push themselves to grow. That message and vision spread throughout the organization via the teams created. Many people grew as managers and leaders in the process, as well as quite a few receiving promotions. One thing was clear. Everyone took ownership in a clear vision.

Whatever vision you and your organization have, in order for it to impact your people and organization, you must define your organization's vision clearly, and then you must get the word out. This involves sharing the vision, so that people want to come along for the ride.

Sharing your vision can be done many ways, and many teams and organizations share the vision for the program through more than one method. In fact, most of the leaders I speak with share their vision and reinforce it every chance they get. Consistent reinforcement of the vision is a best practice for impactful Energy Bus programs. It is like building an internal marketing campaign for your organization. You will learn more about sharing the vision for the road ahead in later sections. Here are some initial examples to give you further fuel for your own organizational road map.

 Best Practices

Desire, Vision, and Focus: Team Tracking Practice

Many organizations maintain regular monthly meetings, and a best practice is to have leaders report progress against a plan in relation to the defined vision. You can put the vision up on a slide during your team meetings, so people stay focused on the goal. You can also have the team provide their updates in the format of a road map. How much of the vision is achieved? Is the team halfway to the vision? Is the team 60 percent there? If the team reports progress on a shared road map, this is another way to reinforce the vision and focus while driving down the road to success together. It will keep you focused together. Some companies take this one step further and publish a progress road map each month to the entire organization.

Case Studies: Sharing the Vision

One CEO opened every monthly meeting by taking five minutes to share the vision. This type of messaging drove ongoing clarity about the destination everyone was driving toward. You do not want to leave it to chance or assume that everyone is aware of the vision. When you share the vision, it is another opportunity to sharpen focus and fuel momentum.

One company hosted an Energy Rally and shared the vision during the rally to kick off their program. The rally was a high-energy event that included an overview of the road map for success and opportunities for reward and recognition for employees as certain milestones were achieved. The more live, interactive, and personal opportunities you can offer to share the vision, the more it comes alive in the day-to-day lives of the group.

Another company rented an actual bus. They loaded up the team and took the bus to an off-site event where the team received information on the vision.

A third company left squishy stress-reduction tools in the shape of miniature buses on all the desks, and then sent a company-wide email announcing a meeting to share the vision. The company's vision was to get through a big organizational realignment, and the stress buses were for the team to use as they sailed through the traffic jams and bumps in the road successfully and with joy.

One CEO depended heavily on videos to launch and reinforce the vision of his Energy Bus program. Each monthly meeting included a video to bring energy up in the room and help people see the vision in action. He said, "We always use a series of movies or motivational video clips to reinforce the vision at our monthly meetings, and we include personal leadership messages from the management team as well."

Vision Consistency

Before every team and organizational meeting share the vision to remind everyone where you are going. This will align everyone and keep them moving in the right direction. You can truly improve clarity of vision, increase motivation and desire, and sharpen organizational focus through this consistent best practice.

When the group knows where they are going, they will know the steps required to get there. Doug Conant, the former CEO of The Campbell Soup Company, told me the most important thing he did was to share the vision. He did it every day, at every meeting, and at every event to reinforce it and make it come alive in the organization.

Rule 3

Fuel Your Ride with Positive Energy

Being positive not only makes you better, it makes everyone around you better.

The fuel that moves you and your team to your destination is positive energy. Real positive energy comes from trust, faith, enthusiasm, purpose, joy, and happiness. Authentic positive energy helps to lead and inspire others. You may have seen amazing leaders help their teams accomplish huge goals. These are people that know how to create and share positive energy; you can feel it when you are around them. The power of positive energy can change lives and the entire world, and it starts with each person fueling themselves with positive energy so they can share it with others.

There is a quote that says, "Where focus goes, energy flows." The practices mentioned in this section of the field guide are all ways to focus on creating that positive fuel. I have a few personal practices that help me start my day with positive energy. One that I recommend is a Gratitude Walk.

I mention it in *The Energy Bus* book and how it provides the right type of fuel for me to be the best leader and driver of positive change that I can be. Here is what I do: I take a nice, brisk walk each morning and make a mental list of all the things I am grateful for. The list is from all aspects of my life, both personal and professional. I think of positive events and people and the many positive occurrences I am blessed by every day. This practice creates positive energy right away. It is a powerful practice in setting me up for positive energy for the day, because it is impossible to be grateful and negative at the same time.

One of the leaders I work with has a plaque on the wall at her home to ignite her gratitude and positive energy. She hung it at eye level in a spot where she will pass by it each morning before heading out the door. It says, "Start each day with a grateful heart." You can take the concept of a Gratitude Walk and create your own triggers and practices to enable you to ground yourself in gratitude each day and create the positive fuel for your ride.

Another simple practice: You can start with a smile. Did you know that smiling increases your serotonin levels? And you can pass that on to others. The recipients of your smile also experience a rise in serotonin and happiness.

Celebrating the successes of your day is another practice that develops positive energy. I ask people to think about what went right in their day. Think about the things that were successes, even if they were seemingly small, or if there was only one tiny thing that went well. When you finish your day, reflect on those positive events. Make a mental list. Run over it in your mind. Through this practice you will inspire yourself to look for more successes the next day—and the day after that. This type of habit gets people addicted to the positive energy.

Another way to foster a flow of positive energy is a practice I call *feeding the positive dog*. I've told the story before about two dogs. One dog represents the negative in life, and the other represents the positive in life. The one that grows is the one you feed the most. You feed the positive dog by focusing on the positive things in life. These would be the things that went well and energize you. When you feed the positive dog, the positive dog gets more prominent in your thoughts and actions. When you *feed the negative dog*, negativity grows inside you.

The more ways you find to develop and nourish the positive focus in your life, the more positive energy and positive fuel you will have for the road ahead. This is the key to fueling your ride.

? **How Do You Fuel Your Ride?**

Complete the questions below.

1. When have you observed positive energy in action? What did you learn from that situation, and how did it make you feel?

_____

_____

_____

2. What does positive energy mean to you?

_____

_____

_____

3. Is your tank full or empty right now? How will you maintain a tank of positive fuel?

_____

_____

_____

4. What energizes you? How can you create practices and habits to reinforce the things that energize you?

_____

_____

_____

5. What are three things you are grateful for? Write them in the space below. After you finish making the list, reflect on the energy you created while focusing on being grateful. What did it feel like?

_____

_____

_____

6. What is one of your recent successes? When you think about your success and focus on what you did right, what happens to your energy?

_____

_____

_____

7. How can you create positive energy by focusing less on yourself and more on others? What are some ways you can shift your focus to making sure to acknowledge someone else's successes? How do you think this will impact your own energy?

_____

_____

_____

8. What one practice will you commit to daily to fuel yourself with positive energy? Track your commitment for three weeks (21 days). Reflect on the impact by writing down your daily practice and the results each week.

_____

_____

_____

How to Help Your Team Fuel Up

There is power in positive people who create positive teams and produce positive results. You have to be energized personally to pass that positive energy to those around you. There are many ways to fuel yourself and then share that with your team.

 ### Fuel Your Ride: Team-Building Activities

$E + P = O$

One of the main ways to help fuel your team with positive energy is to use the $E + P = O$ formula, the Positive Success Formula. Events plus perception equals outcomes. (You can also substitute _positive energy_ for perception if you want to remind yourself that you want a positive outcome.) How you choose to interpret and perceive events will impact the outcome. When you choose to see the opportunities within your challenges, you will enhance your team's positive energy and chance for success. Share this formula with your team, and ask them to discuss how this could help the team create more positive energy.

One team leader introduced this formula to the team by sharing a couple of common events that occurred regularly on the team and asked them to discuss how to apply the formula going forward for the most positive results.

The examples included customer challenges, problems with teammates, and other situations. Once the group reviewed the challenges shared, each person was asked to apply the E + P = O formula to create a positive outcome from the event. The team members shared their examples with each other and discussed how the formula and decision to implement a positive perception produced a positive result. Each month the team was asked to look for examples where this approach was used to solve difficult situations, and the team began to learn from each other. The more the leaders of the team demonstrated their own application of this approach, the more the formula became a part of the team culture. It shaped the way things happened in the team, and it created positive energy to fuel the bus for the road ahead.

You can post examples of success using this formula on a Success Wall where everyone can learn about the positive outcomes that result from the E + P = O equation.

Turning Negative into Positive

Joy from *The Energy Bus* stated a powerful truth, "Where there is a negative, there is always a positive. Where there is a dark cloud, there is always a sun shining behind it." This is another best practice that you and your team can put into practice.

Have each team member identify a challenge they faced in their life and then share what they learned from it and how it helped them grow. Then when something negative occurs, train yourself and your team to be intentional in looking for the positive. When doing this, you do not have to ignore the reality of the challenge. You and your team just need to commit to looking at all situations with an eye for the silver lining. Those situations are where the magic happens and where the most potent positive fuel can be created and shared for your journey.

One team started keeping a list of their monthly challenges, and then the team leader would distribute the monthly challenges in a short email to the team. The team was asked to come up with a short description of the positive they saw in every negative situation. Each month the team came prepared and share their positive perspectives on those tough circumstances. Over time, the mindset became an ingrained part of the team, and they created multiple positive scenarios that could come from their problems. They inspired each other with their innovation and creativity and began to create monthly doses of positive fuel to keep their tank filled with positive energy. This best practice had the team noticing how much positive energy increased, and negative decreased. It changed their team culture.

Read **The Energy Bus** *and Discuss With Your Team*

John Calipari, the University of Kentucky basketball coach, would often read the book with his players and discuss it each week with them. ESPN did a feature on Willie Cauley-Stein and the impact Coach Calipari's mentoring and *The Energy Bus* had on him. It's a great example of what happens when a team reads the book together.

The Positive Pledge Culture Activity

Read the Positive Pledge that appears at the end of this book in the "Keep the Bus Rolling" section. Ask your team, "What would it look like if everyone in the organization adhered to the Positive Pledge?" Individually or in teams, write specific statements about the culture that would result. What might need to change in the culture to create more positive energy? What best practices could be further magnified? Ask the teams to create a visual to represent the culture of an organization if the Positive Pledge was in full effect. Give the group time to complete the activity, and then debrief as a group. Discuss opportunities to act.

Steering Wheel Activity

Gather a team or group together, and share the following statement with them: *Positive thoughts are like the steering wheel that moves the bus in the right direction.* Ask the individuals or groups to come up with thoughts they believe would impact their mental steering wheel to get the bus moving in the right direction for the organization's goals. What positive thoughts help them fuel up and steer themselves and the group? How can the group take action on these ideas?

Safety Zone Activity

You already know the Positive Success Formula, $E + P = O$. This additional activity can take the organizational and cultural impact to an even greater level.

There are many challenges in life and in business. Events can catch you off guard, and the choices you make impact outcomes in a positive or negative direction. The negative outcomes are outstanding learning opportunities, and when you train yourself and your team to apply the Positive Success Formula—even if it results in mistakes—it shifts the focus to solutions for the future, builds trust, and allows the team the space to operate in a Safety Zone, where no one gets run over by the bus.

Each month at your meetings, ask the team to bring some of the mistakes that recently occurred. During a period called the Safety Zone, when no one gets blamed, have the team share mistakes and let the team offer suggestions on how to apply the Positive Success Formula to shift gears toward a solution for the future based on the event that occurred. This activity teaches problem solving and builds trust by not placing blame. It also creates positive energy for the future through the resulting solutions via the Positive Success Formula. It trains your teams on the consistent application of this formula to create positive energy and positive outcomes. You can use the successful turnaround stories and ideas to fuel the team with positive energy. You can also tie some of these solutions to rewards and recognition for solving relevant organization challenges with a positive result. The Safety Zone activity is a fantastic way to train a team to solve problems without a fear of blame or shame for making mistakes. We all know that everyone makes mistakes, and every team needs to understand that reality and figure out a way beyond the need for blame. Blame sucks all the positive energy out of an opportunity for improvement. Having a Safety Zone protects everyone, and it helps everyone become more comfortable asking for, and receiving, help from their teammates.

Creating Positive Progress

Create a list of five challenges that your organization regularly faces. Have your team work in groups of two to five people. Ask the team to use the Positive Success Formula to create the most positive outcome possible to all the challenges listed. Have the teams share their ideas with the group, and choose to adopt some of the ideas as new best practices if appropriate.

These activities all represent simple ways to help teams create positive fuel, and I've seen teams create big, positive change through implementing them and celebrating the positive results. One thing is certain, when teams create, notice, and celebrate milestones on their road map, it creates positive energy. It also increases morale and can increase the organization's brand value in the marketplace.

When you align recognition criteria to the vision for the road ahead, you are reinforcing the vision and creating an exponential amount of positive fuel at the same time.

 How to Fuel Your Organization with Positivity: Best Practices

Once you establish practices for yourself and your team, you may want to look at ways to fuel your organization with positive energy through a more comprehensive Energy Bus program.

 Case Study: Transfer Your Positive Beliefs to Others

When William Bratton took over as police chief of NYC under Rudy Giuliani, crime was prevalent and many people didn't think it could be reduced. Bratton met with his five bureau chiefs one on one and asked them a single question, "Do you believe that you can lower crime in your area?" The two that said "yes" he kept on his team, and the three that said "no" he had to fire. Why play the game if you don't think you can win?

Bratton knew that you have to maintain a fundamental belief and mindset in order to create positive change. That is the type of mindset individuals need who are starting and leading an Energy Bus Program, and it is also the type of mindset that fuels positive relationships, positive teams, and positive organizational outcomes. To fuel your organization with positive energy you must share optimism and belief.

Catch People Doing Things Right

When I meet leaders from all over the world, they tell me that one of the top ways to create positive energy in an organization is to notice what people are doing well. Pay attention to what people are doing right. Look for people doing things right. You create tons of positive energy and fuel by encouraging others in their hard work and achievement. As Ken Blanchard teaches in the *One Minute Manager*, when you catch people doing things right they will do more things right. You can turn this into a recognition program to reinforce the idea that catching people doing things right is a part of the organization's culture. Catching people doing things right is actually the sign of strong leadership.

Chief Energy Officer Awards

Every Energy Bus program I've heard about contained some aspect of recognition of success. One of the most successful car dealerships in the country created a monthly Chief Energy Officer Award to recognize their employees for sharing positive energy with teammates and clients. They found examples that embodied the type of positive culture and values they wanted their employees and customers to feel, and then monthly awards were given to the people who took action to make the car dealership a great place to work and do business.

There are many ways to highlight positive examples, and many of the organizations I've worked with create a formal program and a place to feature the individuals who get the awards. Some organizations put up pictures, some send out emails, some create videos in break rooms, and some use all of these approaches to make sure these successes are a focal point. Focusing on successes creates positive energy and fuels the ride.

Positive Pledge Commitment

The Positive Pledge (see "Keep the Bus Rolling," at the end of this book) is another tool to create positive fuel. One company president asked each member of their team to print "The Positive Pledge," sign their name at the bottom, and post it where they would see it every day. This simple act of commitment to positive energy created a team environment where Positive Energy was considered one of the core values.

Once this action is complete, you can follow up by meeting with your team individually and asking them what they will personally commit to doing in relation to their commitment to the Positive Pledge. Ask each team leader to do the same with their direct reports. Explicitly ask everyone to share any particularly creative or positive actions that are noted during the process, so that the team may implement them on a broader scale throughout the organization.

In summary, I've compiled lists of hundreds of different ways to fuel individuals, teams, and large-scale Energy Bus Programs with positive energy. This Field Guide is my way of sharing success strategies with you and helping to create more positive energy in the world. As you launch your program and implement Rule #3, think about the ongoing ways you will fuel yourself and fuel others. Put those practices in place, and be focused and consistent as you drive down the road towards your vision and goals.

Invite People on Your Bus and Share Your Vision for the Road Ahead

As a leader, you set the tone for your entire team. You must communicate your vision.

—Colin Powell

Positive passengers are wanted. The journey is much more thrilling, full, and rich when it is shared with others. Now that you have a vision to share, you need to communicate that vision and get people on your bus. To get people on your bus, you must communicate in a way that drives alignment and buy-in. I recommend you share your vision with potential passengers, and then invite them on board to join you.

It does not matter how big or how small your goal, your team, or your business is, you need a cohesive and dynamic team to propel your bus to its intended destination. Whether your passengers are your friends, your family, or a workplace team, they must understand and buy in to your vision for the road ahead. A team that is clear on the vision will find a way forward past all the potholes, roadblocks, and delays.

 Questions to Help Get People on Your Bus

Answer the following questions.

1. What kind of vision do you want to share with your team? Is it a personal vision, a family vision, a project vision, a team vision, or a company vision? Write down the vision. Be specific and paint a vivid, verbal picture of the vision you are headed toward.

_____

_____

_____

2. Who needs to be on your bus to be successful? Make a list of the different people that you want to invite first.

_____

_____

_____

3. Based on what you know today, who do you think will get on board? Who may resist? Why?

_____

_____

_____

4. When is the best time to invite someone on your bus? Will you invite your passengers at a launch event? If so, what will that event include?

_____

_____

_____

5. Decide how you will send your bus tickets. Email, printed, or both? (A link to downloadable and email bus ticket templates is provided later in this chapter.)

_____

_____

_____

6. Prepare your vision story to share with others. You can think of it as a vision commercial. Write down your vision and read it to yourself. Ask yourself, "Would I get on my bus? Is this vision inspiring? How can I make the vision more clear and powerful?"

_____

_____

_____

 ## Invite People and Share Your Vision: Team-Building Activities

Share the Vision

Sharing your vision is a simple process that involves clear communication. One of the best ways to get people on your bus is to tell them about your vision, and then ask them to be a part of it. Then, you keep asking.

Joy from *The Energy Bus* said, "Remember, you're driving the bus, George. But as you drive, you want to keep asking people to get on. The worst they can do is say no. If you don't ask, they won't know to get on." It really is that simple to share your vision and invite people to join you on the bus.

How to Invite People onto the Bus

When you share your vision with the group, follow your description of the vision with a specific ask to get people on your bus right in that moment. This is a best practice I recommend. Asking people to join you immediately after sharing your vision is the ideal time to get more positive passengers. This is the perfect time to hand out a ticket and invite people onto the bus.

I created materials to help you invite people on the journey. There are bus tickets for you to give your passengers when you invite them to get on board and be a part of the vision. Sample bus tickets can be found here at http://theenergybus.com/tickets.html. You can pass out the bus tickets when you share your vision, or you can email them. Some leaders do both. Again, the most important thing is to ask, and keep asking. Another best practice I recommend is asking the people who accept your offer to turn their tickets directly back in to you. Turning the ticket back in signifies that they agree with your vision and have a clear desire to be a part of the road ahead. You can offer the group the opportunity to turn in their tickets right away, or you can give them a day or two to think it over and make their decision.

Remember that people want to be invited onto the bus. This can fuel you with confidence in sharing your vision and asking others to be on board. Inviting someone onto the bus makes them feel important, worthy, and valuable. Inviting someone onto your bus tells them, "I want you on this great journey with me. It is important to me that you're with me. Are you in?" People want to be a part of something special, and they want to be included. When you believe in your vision, share it with others, and ask them to be a part of it—you are telling them that you believe in them too. You believe they can make a difference and are valuable to your vision's success. This process is tribal in nature and very powerful.

Keep in mind that you may need to invite people more than once. Maintain a list of the people you have invited and the methods used for the invites. You may want to give people multiple opportunities to accept your invitation. This will also give you plenty of practice in sharing your vision with others and continuing to hone the best delivery of your vision message.

Also, make sure to invite your team on the bus each year. Do not assume they are on it because they were last year.

 Best Practices

Keep Asking

I've already mentioned this, but it is worth reinforcing, that one of the best practices for Rule #4 that I cannot emphasize enough is to share your vision, invite people on the bus, and KEEP ASKING. Many leaders invite people onto their bus and then assume that once is enough. Your passengers need to hear your vision more than once, and some need to be invited many times. Once they get on board, they also need to be invited to stay the course on a regular basis.

Some teams and companies have a re-commitment event on a quarterly or annual basis. They don't necessarily call it a re-commitment event, but they set a time to bring current passengers together.

I recommend this approach. Bring your current passengers together, maybe add some new ones into the group, and recap where the journey has taken you so far. At the event, the driver shares the vision again, and then invites any new passengers on the bus, but also re-invites the current, committed passengers. This helps to keep everyone aligned with the same vision. It also helps the passengers to hear from the driver how much they are wanted and appreciated as a part of the journey.

Be Creative

It may sound obvious, but I wanted to call out creativity as a best practice, because I've seen so much of it with the successful individuals, teams, and companies I've worked with through the years. When you share your vision and invite people to be a part of it, using all your unique talents and creative ideas is a huge asset. It allows you to be *you*. It also highlights the things that make you and the journey ahead so unique. No two visions or journeys are exactly the same, and the way you use your creativity to share your vision and invite people to be a part of it makes a difference.

Every time I think I have seen all the ways to share a vision or all the different types of bus tickets people can create, someone surprises me with something new. This type of innovation energizes me. The creativity is exciting, and it is a best practice when preparing for a launch event, because it is another way to show your passengers how much you care. It shows that you are putting your heart and soul into the vision you are sharing. When people see your creativity in action, it makes an impression, and I encourage you to use your creativity in the way you share your vision and in the way you invite your passengers to join you.

Be Prepared

However you decide to share your vision and invite people to join the journey, make sure you are prepared. The materials on the Energy Bus website and the best practices and examples provided in this field guide were created for a reason. I've seen leaders launch Energy Bus programs for their family, team, or organization in many different ways, and the ones that have practiced sharing their vision and have a plan related to how they will invite their passengers get better results. Those are the type of results I want for you.

You can prepare on your own, or you can bring in other members of your team to help with the preparation. As a best practice, I recommend having a basic plan in place that includes two simple things:

1. Practice sharing your vision a few times before your official launch.

2. Determine what kind of ticket you want to use, and determine how you will distribute the tickets and how they will get turned back in.

Case Studies: Make the Most of Asking with Bus Tickets

I hear from teams and organizations all the time about how they shared their vision and invited people to be a part of it. Many teams and companies use the online resources from the Energy Bus website that I've already mentioned. Quite a few teams and companies customize their bus tickets as well. One thing the successful groups have in common is that they follow Rule #4 by sharing their vision and being intentional about linking the vision to a personal invitation to share the journey for the road ahead. I want you to use all your creativity and passion to share your vision and invite your passengers in a way that fits you. Let your personality and passion shine through. I also want to provide you with best practices from other teams and companies to help fuel your own journey.

Here are some case studies related to how organizations invited passengers.

- A number of schools have handed out bus tickets to their teachers and asked them to turn in their bus ticket and write down why they are excited about the school year on their ticket.

- A college football coach gave his team tickets and asked them to hand them in if they were symbolically buying in to the program.

- A leader of a company emailed everyone in the organization a bus ticket and asked them to print it out and sign it and hand it in at their big company Energy Bus rally.

- Another company leader worked with his marketing department to create a custom Energy Bus ticket with the company mission on the ticket. The tickets were emailed to everyone in the organization and a copy was also posted on a shared location of their intranet. Everyone in the company attended an Energy Bus launch event, where more tickets were printed and handed out, and each employee was asked to turn in their ticket to their manager within two business days of the event if they made the choice to get on the bus.

- One organization had a meeting with all the managers in the company first. The CEO shared the vision with the managers and invited them on the bus. Next the CEO asked the managers to take tickets back to their team and invite them on the bus as well. In this example, the managers got the opportunity to practice delivering the organization vision to their team when they handed out the bus tickets. Everyone in the company was given the same date to turn in their tickets, and after the tickets were turned in, the CEO held an all-company event to share the vision one more time and celebrate everyone that turned in their tickets for the journey together.

- One team took all the athletes out of the gym into the parking lot. The coach shared the vision and invited each person on the bus. As the coach invited each athlete, he handed them a bus ticket. Once everyone was invited, the coach asked everyone that wanted to be a part of the vision to get on a bus that was waiting in the parking lot. As the athletes got on the bus, they handed their ticket back to the coach. Once everyone was on board, the coach took the team out for a team meal to celebrate.

Believe in Your Bus Ticket

This best practice is most effective for larger organizations or teams. Get a trusted group of your senior leaders together before asking the entire team or organization on your bus. Provide samples of the eight bus tickets from the Energy Bus resource page. You can

Invite People on Your Bus and Share Your Vision for the Road Ahead

project them on a screen, print them out, or post them on the walls. Have the group work individually, in pairs, or in teams up to five. The participants should review the eight bus ticket options and determine which one they would recommend to use for your organization when inviting people on the bus to share the vision for the road ahead. The recommendation should be the ticket they believe will do the best job of getting positive passengers on the bus. Give the participants time to review the options and prepare their recommendations. The recommendations and rationale are shared with the group. There are no wrong answers. This activity drives creativity and consensus around the right bus ticket, and it can create a bridge to discuss the invitation process overall. During the initial bus ticket review, the participants can also be given the option to customize their own bus tickets. What you are driving toward is an invitation process that creates the best belief and results to get positive passengers on the bus. I've seen some incredible, custom bus tickets and look forward to you sending more examples.

Rule 5

Don't Waste Energy on Those Who Don't Get on Your Bus

One guy can't make your team, but one guy can break your team.
Spend your time with the people putting in the hard work,
and take responsibility for getting the others off the bus.

—Bill Bottoms, VP of Operations at immixGroup

E ven though you invite people onto your bus, the reality exists that not everyone will want to get on. Not everyone will have the right energy and mindset or share your vision. Some may not want to go where you want to go. Some may even ruin your ride if they get on. Rule #5 states, "Don't waste energy on those who don't get on your bus." That is not always easy, but it is completely necessary to be a successful driver. It is a commitment you must make to your positive passengers. If you invest too much energy worrying about those who do not support or believe in the vision, you'll waste energy that could be fueling your success for the road ahead.

❓ Discover How to Avoid Wasting Energy

Answer the following questions to help you not waste your energy on those who don't get on your bus.

1. Have I truly done everything I can to share my vision and create excitement for the road ahead? Once you can answer yes with confidence, you've taken the first step in preparing for those who won't choose to get on your bus.

_____

_____

_____

2. Think of a time when you wasted energy on a teammate who refused to get on your bus. What damage did this do?

_____

_____

_____

3. What's the best thing you can do when someone refuses to get on your bus? Why?

_____

_____

_____

4. Does rejection hold you back and keep you from taking risks, or does it inspire you to get better? Which is the more positive mindset?

_____

_____

_____

5. How can you not let rejection keep you from asking more people to get on your bus?

_____

_____

_____

Don't Waste Your Energy: Team-Building Activities

See Ya Later

Helping your team prepare for the reality that some people will not get on your bus is a valuable activity. One leader got his team together and asked them to break into pairs to discuss how they would handle it when people did not get on their bus. He called it the "See Ya Later" activity. This was meant in a kind way. It was to deal with the reality that all leaders and drivers have to face: Not everyone will get on your bus.

So, what do you do next? How do you handle it? What do you say? Why is it important to the other members of the team to be prepared for this reality?

In this activity, the pairs discussed these important questions and came up with a short approach for when it's time to say "See ya later" to anyone that decided not to get on the bus. Each pair shared their approach with the team. The team then discussed the different ideas presented and came to agreement on some of the approaches they thought would work best. The result was a few bullets that the team agreed were positive ways to have a discussion when someone decided not to get on the bus. The team said this made them feel empowered and focused on the positive road ahead. This activity also reminded the leaders that they were there to protect the committed, positive people on the bus from the negativity of those who did not want to be there.

Many teams I work with agree that the best approach to this situation is a simple one. You genuinely wish them the best on their journey and be clear that you are letting them off at the next bus stop in a professional and kind manner. Team members recognized the value in being prepared to handle this eventuality with a positive approach.

Right Way–Wrong Way

Another leader got her team together and put them in small groups of three to five. She asked the groups to discuss their positive and negative experiences when someone left a team they were on, or decided not to get on the bus to continue the journey.

The teams can up with a list of three things that were common in their experiences from when things were handled well and three things that were common in the situations where things were not handled as well. Then the teams presented their findings to the group, and everyone on the team was able to debrief and plan in regard to how they would like to handle this situation in a consistent, professional, and kind fashion moving forward.

Using this Rule with Your Organization

Case Study from an Organization

One piece of practical advice for dealing with people that don't get on your bus came from a human resources executive I worked with at a global company going through a great deal of change. Some people on the team were not successful in resolving the traffic jams (disagreement and conflict related to which direction to go) or the discomfort of speed bumps (the change that exists in any growing organization). This executive took a very simple, yet powerful, approach. She asked her teams to intentionally cultivate trust in their organization and their teammates. She asked them to believe the best when changes were made. She also asked the teams to prepare for the fact that some people would not get on the bus toward the new vision, and she let them know that it would still be ok. That they would still be successful.

The leaders in the organization found this to be a very simple and effective way to deal with this change. The people that did not want to get on the bus toward the new vision were communicated with professionally and respectfully. The leaders told them that they wanted people on the bus that believed in the vision, and that was where they would spend their energy. Everyone was able to deal with these situations efficiently and with kindness. Energy was focused on those who wanted to be there to achieve the mission. This energized the dedicated members of the company. All involved appreciated this clear, candid, and professional approach.

The team that wanted to be on the bus stayed, and the ones that did not want to be on the bus found new opportunities. The company went on to hit record revenue and profitability that year. Another benefit from this approach was that these outstanding results gave the organization even more confidence that they had the right team. The process also created more positive fuel going into the next year.

Maintaining Positive Energy When People Don't Get on Your Bus: Best Practices

These best practices are clear and simple, so I'm going to present them as a list:

- Do not take it personally.

- Be Polite. Be courteous. Be prepared.

- Practice how you will handle the conversation when someone decides not to get on your bus.

- Keep it short, and thank them for considering the opportunity.

- Make an effort to have the discussion conclude on a positive note as much as possible.

Post a Sign on Your Bus That Says "No Energy Vampires Allowed"

I will not let anyone walk through my mind with their dirty feet.

—Mahatma Gandhi

I f you want to be successful, you have to be very careful about who is on your bus. Your passengers can increase the energy for the road ahead or drain it. Your job as the driver is to reduce and eliminate any negativity on your bus, and this includes negative people. You must be more positive than the negativity you face and bold and courageous enough to clearly tell people that you will not allow any negativity.

In *The Energy Bus*, I call negative people who drain your energy Energy Vampires. They will suck the life out of you, your goals, and your vision if you let them. They can show up at home, with friends, on your team, or at work. These people just seem to thrive on negativity.

You may know a couple Energy Vampires, or you may even be one yourself. This section of the field guide will help you take action to effectively address the Energy Vampires on your bus.

Let's start by answering a few questions.

? Identify Energy Vampires

1. Before you can work with others' negativity, you must first address your own negativity. Are you an Energy Vampire? If so, are you willing to change? It is a tough question, but you have to examine yourself first.

_____

_____

_____

2. Are there Energy Vampires in your life that are holding you back?

_____

_____

_____

3. What are some ways that you can successfully neutralize them?

_____

_____

_____

4. How do you currently deal with Energy Vampires in your life and on your team?

_____

_____

_____

5. What could you do to improve the process?

_____

_____

_____

6. Are there any Energy Vampires that need to be dealt with right now?

_____

_____

_____

Dealing with Energy Vampires in Your Life and on Your Team

I've noticed that many people can be nervous about dealing with Energy Vampires. I wanted to provide information for you about the great results people have achieved through best practices, and also share some of the mistakes people have made. This way you and your team can maximize the best ideas and avoid the approaches that were not as successful.

The top Energy Bus response to Energy Vampires is to love them. No matter how you choose to deal with Energy Vampires over time, the first response I always recommend is to start by showing them love and understanding, then make an attempt to transform them. No one really wants to be an Energy Vampire, and many times you can have a positive impact on a new approach for these individuals.

Martin, who works for the company Seventh Generation, told me that he put a sign on his door that said, "Energy Vampires welcome. Expect to be transformed." It had a big impact on his team and organization.

The next step in dealing with Energy Vampires is to further open the lines of communication. Most Energy Vampires are usually negative for a reason. Determine if there is a cause for their negativity that you can address. Detail an action plan that will lead to their success and the success of the team. Encourage them to get on the bus with positive energy. Give them a chance to transform and succeed. This shows you truly care, and it can be a phenomenal turnaround story to fuel the journey with even more positive energy.

If the Energy Vampire fails to make changes and, despite your love, support, and planning, continues to be negative, then you have no choice than to ask them to get off the bus. Perhaps there is another bus where they will be a better fit. This may be a tough

Post a Sign on Your Bus That Says "No Energy Vampires Allowed"

conversation, but the journey is too important to be compromised by Energy Vampires. As the driver, you need to be responsible and accountable to this rule.

 ## No Energy Vampires Allowed: Team-Building Activities

Love Letter to an Energy Vampire

This is a great exercise to do with managers. Have each manager write a letter of encouragement to their Energy Vampire. In the letter, write down the positive attributes that person possesses. Find the good in them. Then share your letter with your Energy Vampire. Of course, don't tell them they are an Energy Vampire. We do this exercise in our Driver of Positive Change training program. One time we had a manager share her letter with her Energy Vampire. They talked for two hours and it completely transformed their relationship. It also transformed the manager's leadership style.

Protection from Energy Vampires

Acknowledge to your team and organization that positive energy does not always come naturally for people. Energy Vampires are a reality that everyone needs to know how to address. You all share in the mission of protecting your positive culture from Energy Vampires. One way that organizations can protect from Energy Vampires is to leverage positive accountability partners.

Get the leaders together to discuss this concept, and then have them share this practice with their teams. Ask everyone to find a positive accountability partner. After people find their positive accountability partner, ask them to help keep each other on the positive road by meeting regularly and gently reminding each other when their bus might veer toward the negativity zone. Encourage each other when things go well, and be truthful when your partner may need an "Energy Vampire" alert. The partners protect and train each other, and they are protecting positive culture at the same time.

This is a voluntary activity, but it has formed the foundation for many positive relationships within different teams and companies. I've seen mentor and mentee relationships spring from this approach. I've also seen how this activity can increase team members' comfort with the peer accountability process as well. With this approach, everyone is truly taking ownership of Rule #6 and helping avoid the destructive impact of Energy Vampires.

 Case Study: Energy Vampires on the Football Team

One college football coach needed to address Energy Vampires on his football team. He had all his players read the book and had an artist draw a picture of an Energy Vampire on the wall of their team meeting room. Any time a player was being an Energy Vampire, they put the player's picture on the wall. No one wanted to be on the wall. In essence, the coach was telling his team that we will not allow negativity to sabotage our team and goals. The team lost the first two games of the season, but went on to win the next 10 games in a row and made it to their conference championship game.

I do not recommend business leaders and school officials utilize this specific strategy of singling out individuals; however, I do believe leaders must make it clear that negativity drains others and sabotages team performance—and that is not acceptable. This is a key factor in accountable leadership. Leaders must create a positive work environment where their people can do their best work without being affected by an Energy Vampire.

If you are not in a position to define the culture or hire and fire people, you are likely wondering what the best actions are to address an Energy Vampire on your team or in your office. In this case, the first step is to share *The Energy Bus* book and program information with your manager or leader and encourage them to use it to create positive transformation in your culture.

Energy Vampires: A Word of Caution

You want to be careful that you do not start calling anyone who brings up a problem an Energy Vampire. An Energy Vampire is someone who is consistently negative and doesn't try to solve problems. You want to make sure that people are still comfortable bringing forward challenges so that the team can find a solution. You do not want anyone on your team being called an Energy Vampire just because they have an alternative opinion or are trying to find a solution to a problem through productive discussion.

Dealing with Energy Vampires in Organizations

Most organizations have zero-tolerance policies for things they know put their success at risk. Negativity, complaining, toxic people impact teams, companies, their clients, and financial results. Rule #6 is a zero-tolerance policy for Energy Vampires and a way to promote a positive organizational culture.

I know from experience and the work that I do that not every Energy Vampire is willing to change. If your efforts to transform an Energy Vampire are not successful, and the person is sabotaging the organization, you may want to consult your human resources department for support. There is almost nothing more demotivating to positive performers in any group than a leader saying, "We are charting a course to a positive destination," and then letting individuals who are not in alignment with the vision stick around to detrimentally impact the group's success. As a leader, it is your responsibility to love, transform, and potentially manage out Energy Vampires.

Case Study: Energy Vampire Alert—One Organization's Approach

One company was dealing with the stress of being acquired, and the leadership team noticed that people had started to complain in meetings. The president communicated to the leaders that they needed to keep their teams focused on positive energy and solutions to their challenges. He asked for leaders to issue an Energy Vampire Alert in meetings if the tone of the group veered toward negativity instead of a positive, solutions-driven approach.

By issuing an Energy Vampire Alert, the process empowered anyone to keep the teams accountable to positive and productive meetings. It brought awareness to the need to help protect the positive energy during the changes and challenges that were occurring. When the alerts were issued, it also gave the opportunity for the group in the meeting to take responsibility for the tone of their meetings. It was everyone's responsibility to avoid negativity and energy drain. It became a fun, light hearted way to fuel the road ahead with positive energy and hold everyone accountable.

Positivity and Proactivity

If you do not like the thought of letting people (even Energy Vampires) off the bus at your organization, you are not alone. That is why I always tell leaders and managers about another way to avoid Energy Vampires—one that works before they ever have a chance to start draining energy from the organization. You will not have to let as many Energy Vampires off the bus if you create a positive culture and solid hiring practices from the start. This approach does not guarantee that Energy Vampires won't get into your company, but proactive, positive, culture-building strategies make Energy Vampires uncomfortable, and they usually don't try to get in where they don't fit in.

If the culture of a company is positive, Energy Vampires stick out with their complaining and negativity. They do not like the light, and feel out of place. I've seen Energy Vampires walk themselves off the bus because they did not like complaining alone. Set an expectation in your organization at the cultural level and in your core values that people who drain the energy of others and the organization's vision will not be tolerated.

 Best Practices to Deal with Energy Vampires

1. If you are not a manager or leader and you have an Energy Vampire on your team or in your office, it is also important that you decide to be more positive than the negativity you face. A simple rule is: Your positive energy must be greater than all the negativity. Another best practice is to share *The Energy Bus* book and program

information with your manager or leader and encourage them to use it to create positive transformation in your culture.

2. If you encounter Energy Vampires in your daily life, remember Gandhi's words, "I will not let anyone walk through my mind with their dirty feet."

3. If you have a personal friend or a friend at work who is an Energy Vampire, you may decide to talk to them about their negativity. If you have a strong relationship with them, and they know you care about them, they may be open to your advice. But remember, Energy Vampires cannot see their own reflection. They may not realize they are Energy Vampires.

4. Proceed with caution if you decide to go this route. If you work at an organization, get guidance from your human resources department and training and development staff. And remember, do everything with love.

5. If you have a neighbor who is an Energy Vampire, and it is one of those days where you just do not want their negativity to impact you, it is OK to run away as fast as you can when you see them. You can tell the person that you have dinner in the oven, or that you need to make a phone call. Tell them something that is true, but get yourself away from the negativity in a respectful and diplomatic way. It is OK to wait until the right moment to address the situation.

6. If you have Energy Vampires lurking in your family, I recommend you become a force of positive energy that demonstrates to others what real positivity looks like. Show your positive energy in the form of love, patience, kindness, and care.

7. Smile. It helps keep the Energy Vampires away.

All of these tips are things that take practice, especially in the face of the consistent negativity from an Energy Vampire. I am grateful I can encourage you through this field guide, because I have heard from thousands of people in hundreds of different teams and companies that the results are worth it. And I've seen firsthand how much of a difference facing Energy Vampires can make.

Energy Vampires are not promotable; however, becoming a driver can lead to promotion and greater leadership growth, I tell individuals and teams that another way to help Energy Vampires is to kindly remind them that negativity will halt their potential, reduce the power of their purpose, and generally stall their career.

Over the years, many leaders and their organizations have proven that *The Energy Bus* is an effective tool that creates a common language for organizations to talk about and address negativity, especially Energy Vampires. Chances are you have this field guide because you are already on a positive path. Even so, you may still deal with Energy Vampires and need an approach to be even more effective in transforming them or helping them off your bus.

One of the reasons I put this field guide together is because I have personally observed many organizational transformations simply because an employee shared *The Energy Bus* with a leader, and the leader invited everyone on the bus and addressed the Energy Vampires. I've seen the techniques and best practices provided produce results. Those results have come in the form of personal testimonials, record sales, championship wins, transformed schools, and organizational turnarounds—and many transformed Energy Vampires. The best positive results are what I want for you.

Enthusiasm Attracts More Passengers and Energizes Them during the Ride

Lead with positive, contagious leadership. This is what your team craves.
They want you to lead with heart.

E nergy is contagious! When you are energized about something, it spreads to others. When you are excited about your vision and taking action to make it happen, people are drawn to you.

Being around happy and positive people makes people feel happy and positive. In *The Energy Bus*, the passengers discuss this: "A life touches a life that touches a life. It spreads one person at a time." As the driver of your bus, you spread positive energy through your words and actions on your journey. People can literally feel your positivity, and that is what attracts other positive passengers and keeps them energized as you move toward your vision.

Sometimes people ask me, "How can I exude enthusiasm and energy all the time and also stay real?" I assure them that enthusiasm does not mean you ignore the reality of challenging or difficult situations or act fake. It means you respond to tough circumstances by having enthusiasm and positive energy as a way of life. It attracts others who want to have that as a part of their life too.

You maintain a steady, positive confidence that the world is an exciting place filled with opportunity. By knowing this in your heart, it allows those around you to share in your confidence and be sure that no matter what the issue of the day, you will prevail as you determine to bring positive energy in all circumstances. This type of approach gives everyone the opportunity to find joy and success, even when things are tough. As the driver and leader, you set the tone for this mindset. The positivity increases and takes on a life of its own as more and more people want to join the journey with you.

? Enthusiasm for the Ride

Answer the following questions to keep enthusiasm going.

1. What are you excited about? Write down five things that energize you.

_____

_____

_____

2. What are you enthusiastic about that creates passion and excitement in you?

_____

_____

_____

3. Why are you enthusiastic and passionate about the things you listed? What makes them attractive to you and keeps you committed?

_____

_____

_____

4. How can you share this enthusiasm and passion with others? Write down three ways you can share your enthusiasm about the things you listed.

_____

_____

_____

5. Go back to your vision for the road ahead. How did you describe it when you shared it with others? Is there passion, energy, and enthusiasm in that vision?

_____

_____

_____

6. How can you get excited and enthusiastic each day? How can you bring the passion for your vision into your day-to-day life?

_____

_____

_____

Team Energy and Enthusiasm: Team-Building Activities

Start the Conversation

Keeping the right energy and enthusiasm on your team is linked to team success. As the driver, you should get your team together and discuss team energy. Host a discussion by posing the following questions to the team.

1. Do we need more enthusiasm and passion on our team? If so, what are we excited about?

2. How can we share this enthusiasm and passion with each other in a real and practical way?

Share the Enthusiasm

One leader brought his team together and asked them to write down what enthusiasm meant to them. How had enthusiasm been important in their life?

He asked them to reflect on why enthusiasm was vital for leaders and why it contributes to team success. Each person on the team shared their viewpoint on the questions, and then the team leader hosted a lunch and told each person on the team to tell the person on their left and right how their enthusiasm impacts team success.

The leader told me that the teammates were sharing moments from months and even *years* ago, when someone's enthusiasm had helped keep them focused and energized for success. The team realized that the examples of enthusiasm had kept people from giving up along the journey. Without enthusiasm, the team would have run out of gas.

 ## Best Practices: Enthusiasm throughout Your Organization

Negative people often tend to create negative cultures, whereas positive organizational cultures are created and maintained by positive, enthusiastic people. The leaders and other team members in an organization are the ones who create the atmosphere through their words, actions, and policies. People create the culture. Positive people keep other people at companies.

A basic definition of culture is *how things are done in a particular organization*. To have a positive and enthusiastic culture, you need to have people doing things with positivity and enthusiasm. I've seen organizations accomplish positive culture changes and maintain positive energy through simple best practices.

1. Maintain communication with your employees and be as transparent as possible. When organizations share information, their people feel more connected to the organization and more invested in positive results.

2. Regularly ask for input.

3. Be excited about successes and celebrate them with your team.

4. Give opportunity to people who are committed and demonstrating results.

5. Be fair and consistent in the way you handle roadblocks and other challenges.

Case Study: Enthusiasm and Energy

One organization I worked with wanted their people to bring even more enthusiasm and positive energy to accomplish the year's challenging objectives. The leader of the organization knew that telling the teams to be more enthusiastic was not the best way to achieve this goal.

This leader decided to ask their team how to inject more enthusiasm into the culture. They used online software to ask the team "What would help us add more enthusiasm and positive energy to our culture?"

The team responded with their ideas and had the opportunity to vote for the most popular ideas. By being inclusive and asking the team how to infuse more enthusiasm, the leader created enthusiasm. The ideas that got the most traction were implemented and helped increase engagement on the road to success. Giving your people a voice in the process raises energy levels and creates a "we're all in this together" mentality.

Case Study: Energy Squads and Energy Stations

Another way to empower your teams to bring enthusiasm and energy is by giving them the opportunity to create it themselves. At one company, the CEO asked each vice president to create an Energy Squad for their group. The Energy Squads were responsible for coming up with new ways to bring positive energy. They hosted monthly team lunches, organized team-building activities, and implemented ways for the teams to encourage each other.

One of the ideas from the Energy Squads that really took off was the creation of Energy Stations. The Energy Stations were set up in a convenient location with healthy snacks, Energy Bus posters, notices about people's birthdays, and messages about company successes. Over time, the teams would hang out at the Energy Stations and create even more positive energy through their interactions.

 Case Study: Serve and Get Energized

One company wanted more positive energy, and they did this by taking positive support to their community. Each vice president in the organization asked their department to coordinate a community outreach activity for the quarter. This took place over a two-year period, so all eight departments had the opportunity to coordinate one of the quarterly volunteer events.

Teams were organized and sent on a team bus to volunteer their time for one day at a local charity. This volunteering time was considered paid time off, so the participants did not have to use their personal time off. During the day's event, the teams worked together and also met other community volunteers.

Pictures of the team getting on the bus to ride to the service event and participating in their work for the day were posted on the company intranet. Stories of the experiences and friendships made were shared at quarterly meetings—as were the positive impact to the charities involved. This created internal and external positive energy for the organization and greatly impacted the energy of the entire culture.

Case Study: Innovation Creates Energy

Another company started a program called Driving Innovation. Each quarter employees were asked to submit their innovative new product ideas. The executive team wanted to promote a culture that was energized to produce the next generation of exciting and innovative mobile devices. By asking their employees to submit their most innovative (and sometimes off-the-wall ideas), the company became unified and oriented around a culture of innovation. This led to the belief that they had the talent and drive to come up with the very best market-leading products. Quite a few of the ideas were implemented, and the employees loved being part of the solution. This program became a cornerstone for the company's energized culture.

Creative approaches to cultivating positive energy and enthusiasm can start small and end up making a big difference. The key is to start and get your people involved and energized.

Rule 8

Love Your Passengers

Love is the greatest leadership and team-building principle on the planet.

Y our relationships with people on your bus are everything. You might have heard the saying "People don't care how much you know until they know how much you care." Loving your passengers and investing in relationships with them is a critical component to demonstrating that you care. When people know that you love and care about them, they will want to get on and stay on your bus.

You may be saying, "But Jon, my team passengers are tough to love." Loving your passengers and bringing out the best in others generally begins with believing the best in others, even the ones that are hard to love. This is a phenomenal step that you can take right away. Believe you have the best passengers on your bus, show them you genuinely care about their success, and they will become the best. This approach builds strong, caring relationships that keep the journey positive along the way. When you love your passengers, they know it, and it impacts everyone's results for the better.

? Questions about How to Love Your Passengers

What are some ways that you can make this rule come alive in your life, team, and organization? In *The Energy Bus*, George, the main character, is handed a sheet of paper that lists five ways to love your passengers.

Let's review them here and answer the following questions.

1. *Make time for them.* When you love someone or something, you spend time with them. You nurture your relationship with them. Making time for someone means making an investment in them. Get to know them. Be engaged in the present moment. Really be with that person and focus your energy on them. They will feel the difference.

How will you make time for the people in your family? Your team? Your organization?

_____

_____

_____

2. *Listen to them*. This is not just about an active listening technique. It is about really sitting down and listening with your heart and caring about what they have to say. Empathy is the key. When you ask someone how they are doing, an easy way to show you are listening is to actually wait for the answer and make eye contact.

How will you listen to the people in your family? Your team? Your organization?

_____

_____

_____

3. *Recognize them*. This does not mean trophies or awards. Make your recognition real and personal. Honor them for who they are and what they do. The more people are recognized for doing things right, the more they will do things right.

In what ways will you recognize the people in your family? Your team? Your organization?

_____

_____

_____

4. *Serve them*. Great leaders understand that the higher they get in an organization, the stronger their duty is to serve the people below them, rather than having the people below serve them. The key is to serve their growth, their future, their career, and their spirit so they enjoy life, work, and being on your bus. The more you serve their growth, the more they will help you grow.

In what ways will you serve the people in your family? Your team? Your organization?

_____

_____

_____

5. *Bring out the best in them*. When you love someone, you want the best for them. You want them to be successful and happy. You want to bring out the best in them. Thus, the best way any leader can demonstrate their love for their team is to help each person discover their strengths and provide opportunities for that person to succeed. When you create a system that provides a way for your people to shine, you not only bring out the best in them, but also in others around them as well. If you really want to love your passengers, help them do what they do best. It's that simple.

What will you do to bring out the best in your family? Your team? Your organization?

_____

_____

_____

Case Study: The Impact of Caring

Michael Phelps understands the principle of collective optimism and its impact on caring for his team. In an interview with Bob Costas, he described his approach to taking care of his teammates by aggressively preserving a positive team atmosphere for success before the 2016 Olympics in Rio.

> *Every now and then you hear a bunch of negative comments or someone complaining during training camp. At one of the meetings I said to the guys that we are getting ready to go to the Olympics, this is what we have to do, and if there is a negative comment keep it to yourself. The more positivity we have as a team, the better off we are going to be. As soon as I said that we all became closer, and then we really started getting going.*

When I heard Michael say these words I was thrilled, because in just a few sentences he defined the essence of positive leadership and loving your passengers via authentic caring and accountability to a shared vision of excellence. In the process, Michael shared a truth with the world that I have witnessed countless times throughout the years. A team with talent can be good. But they must come together and truly and authentically trust each other, hold each other accountable to positive results, and genuinely care about each other to be great. Positivity is the glue that enhances team connection and performance. It is the love for your passengers that is at the heart of every successful Energy Bus journey. The concept of loving your passengers and cultivating positivity impacts office teams, school teams, church teams, and hospital teams as much as it does Olympic teams. Many people think that you have to choose between positivity and winning. But the truth is you don't have to choose. Positivity leads to victory. Positivity creates championship teams and organizations. Those teams are filled with people who train themselves individually and collectively to feed the positive and eliminate the negative all through loving one another.

Love Your Passengers: Team-Building Activities

Discussion—Loving Your Passengers

Ask your team "How can we as a team show our team members that we care about them?"

Lead a discussion with the team's answers.

Have one of the team members write down all of the ideas, and send the list back to the team with a note about the importance of caring for team members and reference Rule #8 in *The Energy Bus*.

Another way to approach a team activity is to have each person on the team identify and share one way they are going to love their passengers and put this into practice. Use the chart to map out a plan for loving your passengers.

Ways to Love Your Passengers	Family	Team	Organization	Customers
Make time for them.				
Listen to them.				
Recognize them.				
Serve them.				
Bring out the best in them.				

Trust and Fun for the Road Ahead

Ask your team to work in groups of two or three to discuss the following questions.

Bringing out the best in others begins with believing the best in others and trusting them. How does trust demonstrate love to your team? Why is trust important to team success? How can you help to cultivate trust on your team? What are ways to show your team you trust them?

Have each group share with the entire group. At the end of the discussion, ask for drivers to take action on some of the most popular ideas.

Loving Your Passengers in an Organization

Many times, people will ask me how it is possible to show your team love in a business or professional setting. Leaders at organizations may initially be uncomfortable when I tell them to love their passengers. What loving your passengers really means is making the people at your organization a priority and taking a few genuine actions to demonstrate that you care. Show them you are really doing this together. Make sure they know that you believe their success is your success and vice versa. You can love your passengers in simple, practical ways. In fact, one of the best ways to find out how your passengers would like you to show you care is to ask them.

Organizational Leadership Discussion

Bring organizational leaders together and lead a discussion on the following: How can we show the people in our organization that we care about them?

Case Study: Company Engagement Survey and Recognition Software

One company leader I worked with said, "From an engagement survey we took with National Business Research Institute, we were getting a lot of feedback that people wanted more appreciation. We were struggling on how to do this better. After much thought, we invested in recognition software. Part of the software displays our company values. Positivity wasn't currently one of our values, but we felt it was so important to make it a part of our values that we did. Since launching this software at the beginning of the year, we had over 8,500 transactions. Many of these were directed toward recognizing positivity in the workplace. This has made a significant impact in demonstrating appreciation and loving our passengers in the workplace. It also shows how much we value positivity in our business."

 ## Best Practices

Organizations that have processes or programs to help develop their employees' careers are demonstrating love and caring. Some companies even invest in corporate universities or the Energy Bus "Driver of Positive Change" leadership program.

When companies serve the people who work in their organization with initiatives that enhance their growth, develop their career, and build their future, then their employees will be more engaged!

Leaders need to make the time to serve their employees in this fashion by creating programs that support career development and create paths for the employees to move forward.

It is also important to listen to your employees in order for them to feel loved and heard. Sometimes organizations are too large for leaders to sit down with every employee and listen to their input. One way organizations help make sure their employees have a voice is through an employee survey. You can put together a survey yourself with online tools, or you can partner with a firm that specializes in this field. By asking for input from your entire organization, this process demonstrates you care about your employees' opinions. It does not have to be expensive. It can be as simple as asking, "What do you think will make us even better?" or "What will make things even better for you as a part of this organization?" The most important part of this approach is to address the input provided and take action on some of the best ideas. This will let the employees know you were truly committed to their input and made it a priority to follow up on the information.

Another way to demonstrate love and caring for your passengers is to make time for them. This is true inside small and large organizations. A simple approach is to have managers take the time to do something special with their direct reports once or twice a year. Some companies have the managers take their employees out for a one-on-one lunch or a sporting event or other type of fun activity that the manager knows the employee enjoys. Spending this one-on-one time (that is not a regular work meeting) helps to increase communication and also offers a fresh environment for the manager and employee to build trust.

Love Your Passengers: Make Sure Everyone Feels Onboard

One leader decided to care for his employees and demonstrate appreciation by closing down the office on a Friday morning and taking everyone offsite for a huge company-wide rally. The leader of the program described it this way:

> *I was getting some grief that people were feeling left off the bus. I felt this was a good problem to have but needed to address it and find additional ways to show everyone they were a part of the program and were loved as a part of the team. The executive team supported me 100 percent in taking action. I brought Jon himself in to talk to everyone at the rally. We hired a local celebrity DJ who played really upbeat music. We shared success stories of employees who not only had been impacted at work, but also at home. It was the most incredible experience for the team to see how much they were appreciated and cared for as a part of the organization. It was the first time in our 48-year history that we ever closed the office down to celebrate our team. Additionally, we weren't just celebrating sales, numbers, or growth, we were celebrating our culture and our people.*

Another organization planned a huge party for their team when they achieved a big milestone on their road to success. The leader thanked the team and had a huge cake made in the shape of a bus and gave out awards to people who made significant contributions to the achievement.

One public department in California issued an Energy Bus commendation to driving the success of their Energy Bus program. The commendation included specific examples of the person's contributions to the organization and showed appreciation for the way their behavior impacted everyone around them for the better. This type of thoughtful recognition is something any organization can implement at the individual or team level.

Another way to love your passengers is simply to tell them how much you appreciate and respect them, and keep telling them. One company showed their love for their employees by creating a spot on the company website to post profiles about the employees and explain why they are the heart of that company. Along with the employee profiles, the president of the company made a video of himself talking about the great team they built and how much he loves and depends on everyone in the organization to take care of their clients and the overall business. In the video, he said, "Without our employees, our company could not exist. I truly love each person, and we all work to demonstrate love and caring to each other as well as our clients."

There are many examples of things organizations have done to show their employees that they are valued, loved, and truly cared for. They range from simple to elaborate, but the one ingredient present in all of them is authentic caring for employees' well-being.

Rule 9

Drive with Purpose

Purpose is the ultimate fuel for our journey through life.

P urpose is, quite simply, the *why* behind what you do. Purpose is the fuel for your life and career. Purpose leads you to the future you imagine and the legacy you will leave. Every one of us can find a bigger purpose in our lives and work.

When you are driven by purpose, you are able to find the extraordinary in the ordinary, the passion in the day to day, and the excitement in the simple things. Purpose is not only your road map, but it is also a precious and personal route that takes you to where you are meant to be. A purpose can be short or long term, depending on where you are headed.

Purpose keeps life and work fresh. It keeps you energized when your tank is low and the road is filled with potholes. Purpose drives you forward and helps you lead while growing and learning through the challenges. You are less likely to lose sight of your vision when you have a defined purpose, because when you have a specific purpose, you see the bigger picture. There are many benefits to being fueled by your purpose, and Rule #9 depends on you, your team, and your organization having one in common. Some of the questions and activities below can help you gain even more clarity on your purpose.

Think about Your Bigger Purpose

In *The Energy Bus*, George and his team came up with a bigger purpose for making lightbulbs. Consider what your bigger purpose might be. Your bigger purpose is where you find the most fulfillment. Your bigger purpose is your cause; it's bigger than you alone. Individuals, teams, and organizations can all have a bigger purpose.

If you are a mother, your bigger purpose for your family might be, "To raise kind, compassionate, and respectful children who can think for themselves and stand on their own." A recycling company's bigger purpose might be, "To protect our planet and reduce the amount of trash being piled into landfills."

The bigger purpose is something that can be a lifetime goal. Take some time to reflect.

? Determine Your Purpose

Answer the following questions to clearly define your purpose.

1. Write a purpose statement for yourself and your life. Purpose statements are usually short, succinct, and easy to share with others.

_____

_____

_____

My bigger purpose for myself/my life is:

_____

_____

_____

My bigger purpose for my family is:

_____

_____

_____

My bigger purpose for my work/team is:

_____

_____

_____

 ## Purposeful Team-Building Activities

One Word

An activity that can help you create ongoing focus for your purpose is One Word. This activity came from another book that I wrote with two friends, and it fits well with *The Energy Bus*. The One Word activity helps unlock the power of purpose by giving people focus. Get together with your team and each person selects a word for the year that will give them meaning and mission and passion and purpose. Make a poster to help you connect to the word, and display it someplace to remind you to live it. What one word will you put on the front of your bus to help you drive through life with more passion, focus, and purpose? Imagine if you and your team lived your word for the year. You can read more about this activity, create your own One Word poster, and get a free action plan at www.getoneword.com.

Team Purpose Discussion

You can start with your individual purpose, and you can also identify a purpose for your team. Your individual purpose is one that you carry with you for your personal focus, and a team purpose will drive your team forward. To develop a team purpose, discuss the questions below with your team.

1. What is your team purpose? Your purpose is the "why" behind what you do every day. Discuss this as a team.
2. How can your team live and share this purpose each day?

3. How can you help create team unity and invest in your teammates?

4. What actions can you take to tune out distractions that prevent you from staying focused on the team purpose?

One Word for Your Bus

Many teams turn the team purpose discussion into an activity. I've seen many teams put a large picture of a bus on the wall with their team purpose on it. Then they surrounded the team bus with smaller buses representing the members of the team. Each team member put their individual word on one of the smaller buses. This demonstrated the purpose of the group, as well as the unique individual purpose words that supported the larger team purpose. The visual stayed on the wall for the year and reminded everyone of the overall team purpose, as well as how each of the teammates contributed to the team purpose.

Drive with Purpose

Bring your team together, and discuss the importance of Rule #9 and having a team purpose. Ask them to take some time for personal reflection and then share their individual purpose with the team and how their individual purpose fits into the team purpose. This simple activity creates a way for team members to get to know each other in a deeper and more meaningful way. It also helps the team understand each other better and fosters a spirit of connection through their individual purposes and how they connect to the defined team purpose.

Share Your Purpose

Ask each person in your organization to identify how they are going to live and share their purpose at work. Ask them to write down their personal purpose statement and the company purpose statement. Then on the same document, make a list of specific ways that they will bring this alive within the organization. You can have the employees post their statements on the company intranet or in another shared location. (Posting the plan should be voluntary and optional.) Posting the plan gets more people connected to one another's purpose and the company's purpose.

 Purpose Best Practices

In every organization, there are people who get burned out. Having a purpose for the organization provides the ultimate fuel for a meaningful and amazing journey. This will help people stay on the bus and keep moving forward. One of the best ways to have a purpose-driven organization is to create an organization purpose statement and publish it for all to see. This approach makes the organization purpose a part of the culture.

The best ways to do this include: putting your purpose statement on your organization website, having the purpose statement displayed prominently in all of the office locations, and restating the purpose at all organization meetings and events. When people are aware of the purpose and hear it stated regularly, they will get behind it and feel it come alive through their day-to-day work. You want the people in the organization to know and believe they are a part of the purpose. By keeping the purpose statement front and center, the leaders of the company are showing that they want everyone to be a part of making the purpose a reality.

Passengers Participating with Purpose

One organization asked their employees to specifically contribute to their work each day by bringing a mindset and focus on the organization's purpose. They asked the employees to do this over a three-month period. There were email reminders and other Energy Bus messages about Rule #9 that were sent over the course of 90 days. At the end of the 90-day period, employees were asked to share how this approach impacted them, their teams, and their customers. The stories highlighted examples of increased energy, greater collaboration, improved efficiencies, and a positive impact on customer services.

Whether it is a personal, team, or organizational purpose, read your purpose statements daily, and remind yourself every day why you *REALLY* do what you do.

A Bus with Purpose: Case Study

One leader shared the way *The Energy Bus* impacted their organization and the overall culture

The problem I had in the past, talking culture or attitude or purpose, was that people felt they were being lectured or told what to do and how to do it. The Energy Bus takes this away. It was in front of everyone every day in some way and people couldn't escape from it. We gave out stress buses to put on everyone's desk, we had flyers in the bathroom with positive messages, and we created a Facebook page and invited everyone to connect. The real turning point was when we created a video to support the program and link the program to the purpose of the company. The program made a difference in our company by connecting people together and to the company purpose in a fun and genuine way. It also helped that when we connected employees' individual purpose to the company purpose people stepped up and volunteered to be team leaders or drivers. Over half the bus drivers from our first Energy Bus session have since been promoted to higher leadership positions.

Have Fun and Enjoy the Ride

The goal in life is to live young, have fun, and arrive at your final destination
as late as possible, with a smile on your face.

You only have one ride through life, so you should enjoy it. This is a central theme in *The Energy Bus*, and all of the "Rules for the Ride of Your Life" contribute to leading a purpose-filled and enjoyable ride.

So what are you going to do to make sure you enjoy the ride? Are you going to ride with your eyes closed or are you going to open your eyes, breathe deeply, and be present by taking a look at all the wonderful things that are going on around you? You have to make a choice.

As with other rules in *The Energy Bus*, the approach to Rule #10 is simple. You enjoy your life by knowing your purpose, meeting great passengers, sharing positive energy, giving people the gift of your smile, and radiating love. There is a lot of beauty to see along the way, even in tough times.

One strategy to enjoy the ride is to *slow down*. Slowing down does not mean decreasing productivity. By slowing down you actually increase productivity. When you slow down and take time to enjoy your life and work, you are actually more productive.

Another strategy is to commit to making time for fun. Life is made of memories. When you look back on yours, will it be filled only with stress, or will it be filled with the sweet rewards of enjoying work and life? Commit to fun. It is an important part of enjoying the ride, and you have to make time for it the way you make time for work and other priorities.

❓ Ask Yourself about the Ride

1. What are five ways you will slow down to enhance joy and productivity?

_____

_____

_____

2. What do you consider fun?

_____

_____

_____

3. Write down three things you will do to make your life more fun.

_____

_____

_____

4. Write down three things you will do to make your work more fun.

_____

_____

_____

 **Activities for Enjoying the Ride**

Make Time for Adventure

Identify one action you are scared to take, but if you did, it would enhance your life, career, and/or family. Write down the action and think of a way to turn it into a reality in the next year. What will you have to do to make it possible to take that leap of faith?

The Power of Possibilities

Never stop dreaming. Even thinking of new possibilities revs up the engine on your Energy Bus and helps you have fun and enjoy the process. Think about your biggest life dreams. Write down a list of three of your most exciting dreams/goals. What are some simple steps you can take this year to get you closer to your dreams? When will you put them into action?

    Remember, do not try to drive anyone else's bus, and do not compare your ride to anyone else's journey. Everyone has their own path. Drive your bus with the best of what you have inside, focus on your ride, and *enjoy it*!

 **Best Practices**

Team Fun

When it comes to team fun, the object is to get people talking and feeling the energy. When an activity is focused on getting different people to share their points of view, dreams, and fears, then everyone learns something and the process enriches everyone.

    Many of the team leaders I've worked with find ways to create fun in their day-to-day work, as well as look for ways to create events and celebrations to say thank you, nice work, or just provide time together to enjoy each other. Some teams will have meals together, coordinate a picnic, or volunteer their time. Other ways to have fun on a team can include: making personalized T-shirts, giving each other small gifts, or making sure that everyone on the team knows that having fun while being together is an important and valued component of team culture.

Case Study: Team Time

One leader asked the people on their team to take a different member of the team out to lunch each month. They asked the team to get to know each other better through the lunches and also find out something unique about the team member in the process. Over the course of a year, everyone got the opportunity to spend quality time with each member of the team. At the end of the year, the team leader hosted a group event and asked people to share the things they learned about each other. Everyone enjoyed the process, got to know each other on a deeper level, and they all said they had a great time doing it. The key was that the leader set the tone and supported the team to enjoy team building as a way to create an even more cohesive and enjoyable team environment.

Organization Fun

Creating fun in an organization is very similar to the way you approach fun for a team. Usually an organization is just a larger team, so you need to be a bit more organized in your approach. The first step to having fun in an organization is making sure it is a part of the culture from the top down. Leaders need to be clear that they value fun as a part of the mission of the organization and to communicate that to their people.

Organizations create an atmosphere of fun when they encourage people to have positive relationships and enjoy the people they work with. Doing great work and accomplishing organizational objectives is fun, and the people who do the work need to know they can enjoy themselves in the process.

Who's on the Bus?

One organization set up Energy Stations during their busiest month of the year. The stations had healthy snacks and other small treats for the employees. During the month, different people received recognition through a program called "Who's on the Bus?" awards. The people who were recognized had their picture and a write-up on a poster at the Energy Stations. The other employees were encouraged to write personal notes on the posters and mention positive things about that employee. Everyone had a lot of fun celebrating the successes and writing personal notes to encourage the people being recognized.

 Case Study: Permission to Have Fun

The team at C&A Industries, Inc., a recruiting and staffing company and Best Place to Work winner in Omaha, launched an Energy Bus program that changed the culture. Liz Hall, Executive Director, Training and Development, said

The initial reason I went to The Energy Bus *was that I felt our culture needed a jump-start. It was late in 2014, and I still felt we were a bit sluggish postrecession. Our business was significantly impacted like most everyone else. It was right after our Nebraska Husker football coach got fired. There was plenty of bad news all around, and I happened to catch an article in our local paper from the athletic director at the University of Nebraska that was talking about the culture. His message was all over talk radio, and the message really focused on Energy Vampires and the real reason our coach got fired. I felt there was a direct correlation to what was happening in our business. I will tell you that initially I did ruffle a lot of feathers. People felt it was "soft" and "cheesy." However, because we had such a large pilot group, everybody was talking about it. Because it was a bus, it created so much curiosity, and it gave people permission to have fun, and we hadn't been having as much fun recently. That made a huge difference in bringing life back into the organization.*

Thank you for utilizing this field guide. I hope it encouraged you and energized you and your team. Keep driving with positive energy, faith, and belief. I am sending tons of positive energy your way and am looking forward to hearing your Energy Bus story. You can share it with me at info@jongordon.com. Wherever you are in your journey, the best is yet to come.

Keep the Bus Rolling

Do not follow where the path may lead.
Go instead where there is no path and blaze a trail.

—Ralph Waldo Emerson

As I've mentioned throughout the field guide, it is important to reinforce the Energy Bus principles on a regular basis in order to have lasting impact. Reading the book and answering some questions and an activity is not a one-time event. I know that your work with *The Energy Bus* is the beginning of a positive journey that will change the course of your life, and in this spirit, I want to share some final best practices and materials you can use to create even greater success and an even more enjoyable ride. You can also use these materials as inspiration to create your own ideas and approaches to bolster the success of any of your Energy Bus initiatives. The key is to keep fueling the ride with positive energy.

The Energy Bus Road Map Planning Tool

Job Description for Chief Energy Officer

- The CEO of the Energy Bus program will be the driver and ultimate champion of the bus's success on the way to its destination.

- The CEO must be willing to uphold all 10 of the "Rules for the Ride of Your Life."

- The CEO must be willing to uphold "The Positive Pledge," which appears at the end of this afterword.

- The CEO is the person responsible for successful program rollout, ongoing program management and communication, and tracking program progress toward the destination on the road map.

- The CEO may delegate execution of some of the supporting tasks listed above to Energy Ambassadors, Team Leads, or other types of Bus Drivers, but the CEO is the individual who is committed to getting everyone to the right destination while also creating an atmosphere of fun, joy, and teamwork during the ride.

The Positive Energy Assessment

The Positive Energy Assessment helps you know and understand where your bus is at the start of its journey. That information can help you in designing the best road map to success. As you work through this simple list of questions, consider making a list of the areas of opportunity that you may want to address as you roll out your Energy Bus program.

1. How positive is our culture?

_____

_____

_____

2. How clear is our team in where we are going?

_____

_____

_____

3. How strong is our communication?

_____

_____

_____

4. How connected are we in our relationships?

_____

_____

_____

5. Is our team or company known for being a positive organization to work for?

_____

_____

_____

Energy Bus Planning Road Map

Created by Matt P. Garrepy

As you create your plan, use this road map individually or with your team to support activities, frame discussions, and/or track your progress on the road ahead. You can use these plans as a part of individual development or as a framework to build an organizational Energy Bus program. Use the resource to help the 10 Rules come alive. Be creative. Have Fun. And Enjoy the Ride. You can get a copy of this map at http://www.theenergybus.com/.

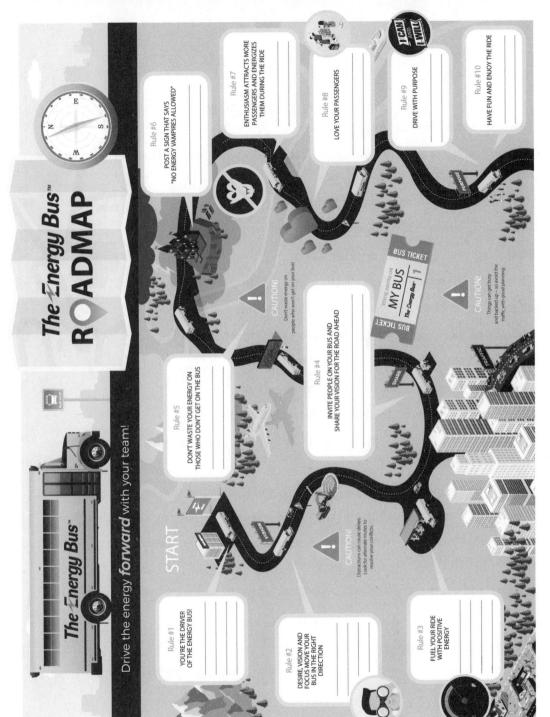

The Energy Bus™ ROADMAP

Drive the energy **forward** with your team!

The Energy Bus™

START

Rule #1
YOU'RE THE DRIVER OF THE ENERGY BUS!

Rule #2
DESIRE, VISION AND FOCUS MOVE YOUR BUS IN THE RIGHT DIRECTION

Rule #3
FUEL YOUR RIDE WITH POSITIVE ENERGY

Rule #4
INVITE PEOPLE ON YOUR BUS AND SHARE YOUR VISION FOR THE ROAD AHEAD

Rule #5
DON'T WASTE YOUR ENERGY ON THOSE WHO DON'T GET ON THE BUS

Rule #6
POST A SIGN THAT SAYS "NO ENERGY VAMPIRES ALLOWED"

Rule #7
ENTHUSIASM ATTRACTS MORE PASSENGERS AND ENERGIZES THEM DURING THE RIDE

Rule #8
LOVE YOUR PASSENGERS

Rule #9
DRIVE WITH PURPOSE

Rule #10
HAVE FUN AND ENJOY THE RIDE

CAUTION!
Distractions can cause delays. Look for alternate routes to resolve your conflicts.

CAUTION!
Things can get busy and backed-up – so avoid the traffic with good planning.

CAUTION!
Don't waste energy on people who won't get on your bus!

BUS TICKET
YOU'RE INVITED ON
MY BUS
The Energy Bus™ 1

The Energy Bus Road Map

111

Keep the Bus Rolling

The Positive Pledge

I pledge to be a positive person and positive influence on my family, friends, co-workers, and community.

I promise to be positively contagious and share more smiles, laughter, encouragement, and joy with those around me.

I vow to stay positive in the face of negativity.

When I am surrounded by pessimism, I will choose optimism.

When I feel fear, I will choose faith.

When I want to hate, I will choose to love.

When I want to be bitter, I will choose to get better.

When I experience a challenge, I will look for opportunity to learn and grow.

When faced with adversity, I will find strength.

When I experience a setback, I will be resilient.

When I meet failure, I will fail forward toward future success.

With vision, hope, and faith, I will never give up and will always move forward toward my destiny.

I believe my best days are ahead of me, not behind me.

I believe I'm here for a reason and my purpose is greater than my challenges.

I believe that being positive not only makes me better, but it also makes everyone around me better.

So today and every day I will be positive and strive to make a positive impact on the world.

www.ThePositivePledge.com

Additional Case Studies

In this section I want to share a few complete case studies with you to help you see the big picture of what an Energy Bus initiative in an organization looks like and the difference it makes. These are just a few of the many stories that have been shared with me, and I hope they encourage you to create your own Energy Bus program. If you do, please let us know how it goes. We would love to hear from you and even include you in future revised editions of the Field Guide. Thank you! I'm sending positive energy your way.

Precyse: Take a Ride on The Precyse Energy Bus

Precyse is delivering new energy, insight, and technology in a new era of healthcare. We address complex issues with robust, nimble solutions and services that transcend challenges and transform workflow. Precyse has enabled more than 1,000 hospitals and health systems nationwide to improve efficiency and deliver tangible outcomes through our advanced proprietary software and services for more than a decade. Visit us at www.PRECYSE.com.

Despite Greyhound's attempts at using a sleek gray race dog in their brand, it's unlikely that many of us think of a bus as the most efficient or fun way to travel. That didn't stop Precyse President and Chief Energy Officer Chris Powell from encouraging his colleagues to take a ride on *The Energy Bus*. He knew only too well that in today's healthcare climate nearly everyone could use a dose of positive energy. And so *The Energy Bus* pulled into Precyse in spring 2012 amid a fanfare of interest and enthusiasm.

Precyse started this journey by illustrating to our senior leadership how each of the ten rules of *The Energy Bus* aligns with our visions and values. The campaign continued by introducing all Precyse colleagues to the tenets of *The Energy Bus* via bi-monthly internal eBlasts from Chris. The 10 Rules for the Ride of Your Life that George learns were explored in subsequent issues. It wasn't long before colleagues were asking, "Where's the ticket window?" and "How do I ensure my seat on the Precyse Energy Bus?"

Chris encouraged everyone to develop a personal Energy Bus action plan and to solidify those plans by writing down their vision or purpose statement and sharing it with their team. He also encouraged active visualization for ten minutes each day to determine which action steps they would take to achieve their goals. The executive leadership team implemented a Friday morning energy deposit call, which Kristen Saponaro, vice president, marketing, says ". . . helps us build off of each other's momentum. The energy derived from sharing our successes every week launch us into our next round of priorities with renewed vigor and enthusiasm."

Lending libraries were set up in the Philadelphia and Atlanta area Precyse offices so that anyone could borrow *The Energy Bus* or a number of Jon's other books. Visits to www.TheEnergyBus.com were noted and snippets from *The Energy Bus* were mentioned during our quarterly Town Hall all-employee webinar. A Precyse Energy Bus mural that is part chalkboard was painted on the wall of one of our offices, enabling colleagues to write energy deposits on it with chalk. And a special "Precyse Bus" hyperlink was created for our internal website that took visitors to a video of Jon Gordon presenting at the managers' meeting.

Chris encouraged colleagues to email him with their vision and ideas for building positive energy and enthusiasm. The Vice President of Product Management & Strategy, Dee Lang, responded by ordering *The Energy Bus* for each member of her team and introduced daily 15 minute GET-ENERGYZED sessions where everyone makes an "energy deposit" such as recognizing a team member or sharing positive feedback from a Precyse colleague/client. The only "rule" was that there were to be no backward steps and no energy vampires. Lang also sent her team a link that takes them to a ticket to get on her bus. Lang's required reading assignments and her team's acceptance of the ticket demonstrated to her that her passengers really wanted to "be on the BUS"!

At the annual managers' meeting, Precyse showed they were thinking bigger than ever. In fact, if the Precyse bus were a hybrid, you'd say we're fully charged and we're not stopping! In the driver's seat was Jon Gordon, our keynote speaker, special guest, and the author of *The Energy Bus*! Hearing Jon speak live and take what we read to the next level was phenomenal! Afterward, Chris highlighted some of Jon's talk that resonated with him, particularly in the areas of optimism, connecting, and engagement.

Optimism. If we build a Precyse culture based on optimism we will be personally equipped with a distinct market advantage that will drive our financial success. By employing a positive, strong, and grateful heart where we choose hope, not fear, we can achieve greatness, individually and as a corporation.

Connecting. We have to connect personally and professionally to build the trust that will sustain us as we work through challenges. So instead of thinking that we're working alone, let's focus on communication, coaching, and caring for each other, because we're all in this together.

Engagement. While "balance" has been a hot topic in corporate America over the past 20 years, Jon suggests that it's more about finding a rhythm that works for you and your work situation. Design the best life where you can optimize your focus and stay engaged.

At Precyse, we have developed our energy action plans. We have posted our "No energy vampires allowed" reminders. We have filled our seats on the Precyse energy bus with like-minded passengers. Together we have created a vision and defined what success looks like for us, our teams, and Precyse. We put our faith in the right things and are learning to trust ourselves and each other. We love the passengers on our bus. We don't come to work every day just to do a job; we come to continue our mission. And we THINK BIG.

Even if you never have the opportunity to meet Jon Gordon personally, you probably feel like you already know him. You have not only read his words, but you have applied them to your lives. I promise you, his enthusiasm and positive outlook are contagious and they are traveling the halls of Precyse . . . catch some Jon Gordon today!

BONA: How One Company Utilized *The Energy Bus* to Create a Positive Culture and Grow Their Business

Since 1919, Bona has provided professionals with premium quality finishing systems and cleaning products developed to maintain the natural beauty of wood floors. With global headquarters in Malmö, Sweden, and subsidiaries and distributors in over 50 countries, Bona leads the industry worldwide with innovative, environmentally responsible solutions to a formerly hazardous and toxic process. The pioneer of waterborne finishes and dust containment in the industry, Bona provides the cleanest, most convenient and healthiest hardwood floor finishing process available. As a privately owned, mid-sized company with solid revenues and growth, Bona prides itself on quality products, produced from an outstanding research and development team. In addition, Bona's recent expansion into mass retail with floor care products has created tremendous opportunities into new, profitable territories. Approximately 120 employees are located in the US and about 450 worldwide.

www.Bona.com

Regardless of the economic times, 2008 started out on a positive note for Bona US. At the yearly sales meeting in Aurora, Colorado, Bona's focus was on planning and advancing, while concentrating on their core values for health, the environment, and exceptional customer service. A few weeks prior, Barry Sopinsky, Bona's director of sales, had just finished his copy of Jon Gordon's international bestseller, *The Energy Bus*. He was truly inspired, to say the least, and decided to propose having Gordon come speak to the entire Bona Team. And so it came that the first invitation to ride the bus was extended by Sopinsky . . . and accepted by the Bona Executive Team. Gordon spoke to the Bona sales team that year, and became quite familiar with the Bona community. During his presentation, he focused on his 10 rules for positive energy and explained the road map to navigate the negativity and pitfalls associated with challenges and adversity in business and life. Gordon's presence was uplifting and extremely motivational through his easily relatable stories and experiences. He gave everyone a new perspective on positive thinking personally and professionally.

In fact, the impact Gordon had on individuals and the executive team at Bona was infectious. Managing Director John Rauvola decided to stay on board Gordon's Energy Bus by giving each employee a copy of *The Energy Bus* and holding company success meetings every month. With the help of Bona's marketing and graphic design team, a company vision for 2010 was created that included a logo and company timeline to track successes along the journey to reaching Bona's goals. By capturing sales objectives by month on the "Sales Expressway," "Operating Income Ave.," and "Gross Margin Blvd.," inspiration ensued with each employee at work by visibly watching the company meet their goals throughout the year. Each success meeting also presents an opportunity for all employees from each department to share recent successes they have had over the last month.

After the first company success meeting, each employee was given a Bona Bus Ticket and color-coded name tag to embark on a journey of team building, fun, prizes, and excitement. After being shuttled to Amazing Jakes, an indoor fun factory full of rides, attractions, and food, Bona employees were split into teams and challenged to the ultimate scavenger hunt. The day gave employees the chance to get to know each other on a more personal level by working as a team and challenging themselves to interactive tasks, such as go-karts, laser tag, and a climbing wall. A definite positive energy presided over the day and helped move the Bona Bus further in the right direction.

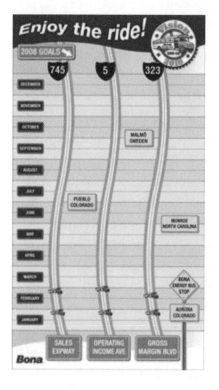

Bona also invited Gordon to speak to their customers at their Distributor Executive Conference and again at the annual sales meeting in February. It is evident that his words and contagious inspiration have created a new and unique culture at Bona. It shows in the attitudes of the employees and in the success of the company through dedication and lots of hard work. Constantly bombarded with negative news and a sinking economy, Bona had a choice between two roads and they chose to keep driving their bus through it all with a clear, positive vision ahead.

Rauvola states, "Exercising Jon Gordon's positive message in our personal and professional lives is extremely important to maintain a successful company. Positive energy passed between employees encourages stronger work ethic and an end result of increased productivity. We hope everyone stays on board the Bona Energy Bus because we are too blessed to be stressed."

The Planes Companies packs all of the services needed for relocation in one company. Their objective is to develop and maintain permanent relationships with their customers by providing outstanding service move after move, with no exceptions. Their goal is complete customer satisfaction. They pledge to find a way to exceed customer expectations, no matter how great the challenge; to stand behind every service commitment; and to employ friendly, skilled, knowledgeable people who, in the event of a problem, will do whatever is necessary to make things right—right away. Their training programs and day-to-day procedures are built around doing what it takes to provide the best relocation services in the industry, and do it with integrity.

The Planes Companies uses *The Energy Bus* to bring positive energy into the organization, while driving business performance and changing leadership behavior. Everyone in the Cincinnati corporate headquarters read the book. That is over 250 team members. As a part of the initiative, each team member had a conversation with their supervisor about the book. They asked things like "Are you more like George or Joy?" "Which rule had the most impact on your life?" "How could each team member apply what they learned to what we do at work?"

To celebrate the initiative, the company hosted an "Energy Bus Day" on May 4, 2017. Activities included giving everyone who read the book a Planes bus ticket, having everyone sign a large Energy Bus sign that stands in the lobby today, and having food trucks visit the building for every team member to get a complimentary lunch. The company integrated the core principles of TEAM (trust, empowerment, accountability, mesh) with the Energy Bus program, and continues to reinforce the positive business outcomes with further activities. The rules in the book have inspired many of the team members. The Claims Team wrote an original Energy Bus Rap and put it to music in a leadership meeting. The Customer Service Team created their own team program with a unique approach to battle negativity through their Energy Vampire call outs. The company has definitely changed for the better, and the leaders at Planes say that this has impacted people personally, as well as hit the bottom line results.

PLANES
COMPANIES

ENERGY BUS RAP SONG

Claims Team – a.k.a. Run AMC

PLANES
COMPANIES

ENERGY BUS RAP SONG

Claims Team – a.k.a. Run AMC

Additional Case Studies

PLANES COMPANIES

ENERGY BUS DAY SIGNAGE & EMAIL

PLANES COMPANIES

ENERGY BUS DAY

Marketing Team

NO ENERGY VAMPIRES ALLOWED

Residential Customer Service Team

7

ENERGY BUS FOOD TRUCK CELEBRATION

Planes Companies Cincinnati, OH

6

THE
ENERGY BUS
TRAINING PROGRAM

A TRAINING TOOL TO FUEL YOUR LIFE, WORK, AND TEAM WITH POSITIVE ENERGY

The Energy Bus Training Program is an innovative online training platform to help you and your team harness the power of positive energy.

- A 60-minute course featuring an **animated video** retelling of *The Energy Bus* story, and video commentary by Jon Gordon himself
- Interactive exercises tied to each module
- A customized action plan to help you implement Jon Gordon's 10 Rules and fuel your life, work, and team with positive energy
- Lessons to enhance your positivity and performance
- Management tools to organize and track the progress of your team

Powerful. Scalable. Enjoyable. **The Energy Bus Training Program** is an energizing vehicle for transporting your organization to new heights of accomplishment.

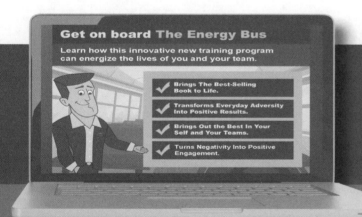

Get on board The Energy Bus

Learn how this innovative new training program can energize the lives of you and your team.

✔ Brings The Best-Selling Book to Life.

✔ Transforms Everyday Adversity Into Positive Results.

✔ Brings Out the Best In Your Self and Your Teams.

✔ Turns Negativity Into Positive Engagement.

Get on The Bus today!

You and your team will be glad you did.

Learn more at **energybustraining.com**

WILEY

If you are interested in contacting Jon Gordon and his team, please contact The Jon Gordon Companies at:

Phone: 904-285-6842

Email: info@jongordon.com

Online: JonGordon.com

Twitter: @JonGordon11

Facebook: Facebook.com/JonGordonpage

Instagram: JonGordon11

Sign up for Jon's weekly positive tip at: JonGordon.com.

Acknowledgments

Jon Gordon

I want to thank Amy Kelly for her tireless effort in making this Field Guide a realty. I couldn't have done it without her help. I thank her family for supporting her as she invested time to work on this field guide with me. I thank my family for their continued love and support. I thank the amazing team at Wiley and all the people and organizations that shared their stories with us. Amy lists these people and companies and I want to add another big dose of gratitude to her words.

Amy P. Kelly

I am grateful for the opportunity to write this field guide with Jon and the amazing team at Wiley. The entire project was (is) fueled with incredibly powerful positive energy.

Thank you to Jimmy Page for the introduction to Jon Gordon and for being a huge part of the power of positive energy in our world.

Thank you to all the company leaders, team leaders, and families that contributed personal time and examples to this first edition of the Field Guide. There are so many that shared invaluable input and personal stories. A particular thank you to the Planes Company CEO John Sabatalo, his Sr. VP of Strategy and Marketing David McGlynn, and all the employees at Planes. Their generosity to share their story and spread their positive energy for others to benefit was a gift. Thank you to Liz Hall from C&A Industries. Her insights and innovation with the Energy Bus provided immense value in this process and are still an ongoing shining example. Thank you to everyone at C&A that made their Energy Bus program a huge success. Thank you to President and General Manager David Stewart and the entire team at immixGroup that drove the Energy Bus to record success, especially ReLita Clarke for her partnership and commitment to the Positive Pledge and the role of Training and Development in spreading positive energy in companies and teams. Thank you to Matt Garrepy. His talent to help translate people's purpose and vision into gorgeous art and design is unparalleled.

Thank you to my family. My husband Jim and children Patrick, Natalie, Daniel, and Samuel. You all understand the power of gratitude, encouragement, and positive energy as we drive as a united family of Energy Bus drivers that never give up. Thank you to my mom Lois Jenkins Jancaitis in heaven and my other moms who have poured positive energy into the world for my entire life. It is always a gift to have people believe in your wildest dreams and encourage you to Be a Driver: Aunt Lorraine, Betty Moore, and Judy Kerr-Greenbaum. Thank you to my pastors Charlie and Jill Whitlow and Fred Vann. The positive energy that we believe in is the strongest available, and you share it generously with all you encounter.

Lastly, thank you to Jon Gordon. Your belief and love of people and the power they have inside them to do great things through positive energy is a belief I share, and you are a leader who will continue to impact the world for the better. May this Field Guide be a huge part of that for millions of people. Thank you for your positive heart.

Other Books by Jon Gordon

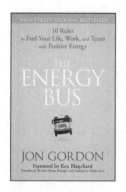

The Energy Bus

A man whose life and career are in shambles learns from a unique bus driver and set of passengers how to overcome adversity. Enjoy an enlightening ride of positive energy that is improving the way leaders lead, employees work, and teams function.

www.TheEnergyBus.com

The Energy Bus for Kids

The illustrated children's adaptation of the bestselling book, *The Energy Bus*, tells the story of George, who, with the help of his school bus driver, Joy, learns that if he believes in himself, he'll find the strength to overcome any challenge. His journey teaches kids how to overcome negativity, bullies, and everyday challenges to be their best.

www.EnergyBusKids.com

The No Complaining Rule

Follow a VP of Human Resources who must save herself and her company from ruin, and discover proven principles and an actionable plan to win the battle against individual and organizational negativity.

www.NoComplainingRule.com

Training Camp

This inspirational story about a small guy with a big heart, and a special coach who guides him on a quest for excellence, reveals the eleven winning habits that separate the best individuals and teams from the rest.

www.TrainingCamp11.com

The Shark and the Goldfish

Delightfully illustrated, this quick read is packed with tips and strategies on how to respond to challenges beyond your control in order to thrive during waves of change.

www.SharkandGoldfish.com

Soup

The newly appointed CEO of a popular soup company is brought in to reinvigorate the brand and bring success back to a company that has fallen on hard times. Through her journey, discover the key ingredients to unite, engage, and inspire teams to create a culture of greatness.

www.Soup11.com

The Seed

Go on a quest for the meaning and passion behind work with Josh, an up-and-comer at his company who is disenchanted with his job. Through Josh's cross-country journey, you'll find surprising new sources of wisdom and inspiration in your own business and life.

www.Seed11.com

One Word

One Word is a simple concept that delivers powerful life change! This quick read will inspire you to simplify your life and work by focusing on just one word for this year. *One Word* creates clarity, power, passion, and life-change. When you find your word, live it, and share it, your life will become more rewarding and exciting than ever.

www.getoneword.com

The Positive Dog

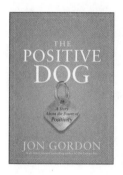

We all have two dogs inside of us. One dog is positive, happy, optimistic, and hopeful. The other dog is negative, mad, pessimistic, and fearful. These two dogs often fight inside us, but guess who wins? The one you feed the most. *The Positive Dog* is an inspiring story that not only reveals the strategies and benefits of being positive, but also an essential truth: being positive doesn't just make you better; it makes everyone around you better.

www.feedthepositivedog.com

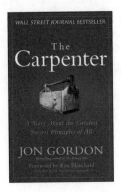

The Carpenter

The Carpenter is Jon Gordon's most inspiring book yet—filled with powerful lessons and success strategies. Michael wakes up in the hospital with a bandage on his head and fear in his heart after collapsing during a morning jog. When Michael finds out the man who saved his life is a carpenter, he visits him and quickly learns that he is more than just a carpenter; he is also a builder of lives, careers, people, and teams. In this journey, you will learn timeless principles to help you stand out, excel, and make an impact on people and the world.

www.carpenter11.com

The Hard Hat

A true story about Cornell lacrosse player George Boiardi, *The Hard Hat* is an unforgettable book about a selfless, loyal, joyful, hard-working, competitive, and compassionate leader and teammate, the impact he had on his team and program, and the lessons we can learn from him. This inspirational story will teach you how to build a great team and be the best teammate you can be.

www.hardhat21.com

You Win in the Locker Room First

Based on the extraordinary experiences of NFL Coach Mike Smith and leadership expert Jon Gordon, *You Win in the Locker Room First* offers a rare, behind-the-scenes look at one of the most pressure-packed leadership jobs on the planet, and what leaders can learn from these experiences in order to build their own winning teams.

www.wininthelockerroom.com

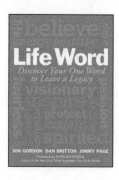

Life Word

Life Word reveals a simple, powerful tool to help you identify the word that will inspire you to live your best life while leaving your greatest legacy. In the process, you'll discover your *why*, which will help show you how to live with a renewed sense of power, purpose, and passion.

www.getoneword.com/lifeword

The Power of Positive Leadership

The Power of Positive Leadership is your personal coach for becoming the leader your people deserve. Jon Gordon gathers insights from his bestselling fables to bring you the definitive guide to positive leadership. Difficult times call for leaders who are up for the challenge. Results are the byproduct of your culture, teamwork, vision, talent, innovation, execution, and commitment. This book shows you how to bring it all together to become a powerfully positive leader.

www.powerofpositiveleadership.com

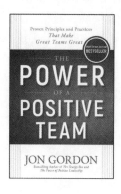

The Power of a Positive Team

In *The Power of a Positive Team*, Jon Gordon draws upon his unique team building experience, as well as conversations with some of the greatest teams in history, to provide an essential framework of proven practices to empower teams to work together more effectively and achieve superior results.

www.PowerOfAPositiveTeam.com

The Coffee Bean

From bestselling author Jon Gordon and rising star Damon West comes *The Coffee Bean:* an illustrated fable that teaches readers how to transform their environment, overcome challenges, and create positive change.

Thank You and Good Night

Thank You and Good Night is a beautifully illustrated book that shares the heart of gratitude. Jon Gordon takes a little boy and girl on a fun-filled journey from one perfect moonlit night to the next. During their adventurous days and nights, the children explore the people, places, and things they are thankful for.

The Hard Hat for Kids

The Hard Hat for Kids is an illustrated guide to teamwork. Adapted from the bestseller *The Hard Hat*, this uplifting story presents practical insights and life-changing lessons that are immediately applicable to everyday situations, giving kids—and adults—a new outlook on cooperation, friendship, and the selfless nature of true teamwork.

www.HardHatforKids.com